Wisdom With Understanding is Better Than Rubies

Lurine Karon Greenberg
Fine Arts Collection

Ethical BUTCHER

Ethical BUTCHER

How Thoughtful Eating Can Change Your World

BERLIN REED

Soft Skull Press
an imprint of COUNTERPOINT | BERKELEY

Library of Congress Cataloging-in Publication is available.

ISBN 978-1-59376-505-7

Cover Design: Jeff Miller at Faceout Studio
Photography: Alison Picard
Interior Design: Sabrina Plomitallo-González,
Neuwirth & Associates

Soft Skull Press
An Imprint of Counterpoint
1919 Fifth Street
Berkeley, CA 94710
www.softskull.com

Printed in the United States of America
Distributed by Publishers Group West

10 9 8 7 6 5 4 3 2 1

For Jackie, my partner-in-revolution~
In you I have found a graceful fighter who understands the value of looking fly while changing the world. It is my pleasure to say my dream girl is a Nightmare Woman. Here's to shaking the world until there's room for everyone.

For Daviana~
From the first time I held you, I knew you were a gift from the stars. Be unapologetic in your uniqueness, do whatever makes you feel whole, and never listen to people who stopped dreaming long ago. This world is yours.

For my Oma~
Nothing in my life would have been possible without the love, guidance, protection and hope that you've given me.
You taught me to be brave, proud and honest and most thankfully, to enjoy feeding the hearts of the ones I love and pour myself into my work.

You've always asked me to write your life story,
I promise this is only the beginning.

For Angela, Ally, Mieke, Simona, and Jessie ~
In vastly different ways, you have each left indelible imprints on my road map.

I am thankful for your light along the way, for I would have been lost without it. Our paths may have diverged, but I am assured of the worth of our encounters. I hope that your travels lead you to the fulfilled destiny for which your talents have prepared you.

and

In lasting memory of Tupac Amaru Shakur.

TABLE OF CONTENTS

FOREWORD

In archetypal terms, Berlin Reed is a Seeker—someone who always believes it is possible to find a deeper level of truth and a truer expression of that truth. This spirit guides Berlin's work and his very unusual path. This book explains a lot of what Berlin thinks and a lot of what Berlin does and leaves us anxious to share who Berlin is. But the best way for us to say that is to share a bit of the context for Berlin, which will hopefully say something true about him.

We are the founders of The Butcher's Guild. Our membership is a national network of butchers (duh) who practice whole animal butchery. This means they buy meat in an entire carcass with some regularity to prepare in their restaurants or to sell in their shops or at a farmer's market. And in our prefab food industry, if you are buying a whole carcass, it probably means you are buying from a local farm. So our members also tend to be advocates for rich, local food communities. They generally know the names of the ranches in the area; they can tell you what squashes are in season or how the weather has affected their watershed. They are sensitive butchers in the sense that they are sensitive to their place in an environment and a community. Their work is bigger than a paycheck; it means more than showing up. And Berlin may be the most sensitive of all these sensitive butchers.

In the Seeker spirit, Berlin is a bit of a wanderer. We have shared meals together in Portland; San Francisco; New York; Grass Valley, California; and in rural southern Oregon. He has committed years to connecting this idea of a context to food by showing people their own beauty. Part of the pleasure of community is that it makes it obvious what you have to share. When Berlin hosts an event, it is a gathering centered on the food producers and craftspeople, generally in their own sweet settings. Sometimes the guests have provided meat; sometimes an herb liqueur. Often they bring their appreciation. When you are raising pigs or are behind a kitchen door all day, to be seen and thanked and reveled in is a quenching experience. Berlin exhibits a raw generosity of the limelight; he's both a star and a supporting character all at once. As people who find our own deepest joy in helping others shine and connect, we see a kindred soul in Berlin's instincts.

Food is the subject, the object, the verb. It is our lens. It is Berlin's megaphone. In many ways, he is the most radical of our members and our friends. But in the universal, deep-down way, he is simply using food to tell you that you are beautiful and you are the truest expression of this beautiful earth.

Marissa Guggiana and Tia Harrison
Cofounders of The Butcher's Guild
November 2012

INTRODUCTION
Begin with Billy

My hand was steady, but my head was spinning. Billy's eyes were two fixed, cloudy marbles. I traced the topography of the outstretched goat carcass before me with my eyes, then with my hands. When you are so acutely aware of every choice that led you to the present moment, thoughts swirl in the mind. In these moments, for better or worse, we are made most human. The air is charged with energy, caught somewhere between construction and destruction. *Kairos*. The ancient Greeks used this word to distinguish these watershed moments from *chronos* and its linear description of time. Billy pushed me onto a path I didn't know I was looking for, and even as I stared into his glazed gaze knowing I was in for a transformation, I had no idea this path existed or where it would lead me.

Just a couple of weeks earlier, my mentor butcher, Bryan Mayer, and I had cut the first whole animal we had ever bought for the shop we ran in Fort Greene, Brooklyn. We had chosen a goat as our first foray into whole animal butchery because it was something new for our customers, who were used to the common selection of beef, pork, and chicken. Goats appeared to be an accessible challenge for us, two new butchers who had never cut any whole animal larger than a chicken. These young goats seemed like an easy feat for a couple of first-timers.

Bryan and I had a brotherly learning dynamic, as he had begun butchering only months before I did. We both fell in love with butchery and spurred each other on in our learning. For days we had been using "Cabrito!"— Spanish for goat kid—with each other as a greeting. Exuberantly obnoxious high fives were often involved.

While Bryan sharpened the knives and cleared our work space, I ran down to get our goat friend. Like most New York food businesses, our storage was downstairs, under those death trap steel doors in the sidewalk. Trudging up and down stairs carrying a 110-pound beef leg on my shoulder, I'd startle even hardened Brooklynites as I emerged from the basement, weaving through pedestrians walking to and from the C, F, and G trains, all of which had entrances just feet away from our door. Though less imposing, the slack-tongued goat carcass got even more horrified amusement than the gams of beef usually commanded.

As was typical for the days when Bryan would teach me

a new technique, I sat on the counter behind him, craning and stooping to see as he cut and talked. This often meant that I learned new techniques by either peering down from my perch above his shoulders or peeking below when I could see into that triangle of space between his arms and torso. In this case, as Bryan was learning as he cut, it was more of the mystified blind leading the mystified blind. I can't honestly say that I saw too much that day, but our shared enthusiasm at just the presence of this carcass was transformative. Once Bryan had made it through the cutting, we were both so excited about this milestone that we agreed the skull had to be saved for posterity. It was rightfully his, since he had done the cutting and dreamed of making a goat head cheese. Lucky for me, though, he was planning to leave the city for a few days and agreed to let me keep the skull.

Up to this point, I had worked only with fish, whole chickens, and primal cuts. After watching my first carcass become leg roasts and loin chops, I was eager to memorialize the change I felt coming over me. The very next day, I embarked on my first of several major *holy-hell-I-am-not-a-vegetarian-anymore* projects: bone preservation.

The mini fridge, or lowboy, as we call it in the kitchen, was where we kept things for quick access. I scanned the lowboy's paper-wrapped packages, passing over Sharpie-penned labels saying "T Round" and "b/o loin," "s rib-marinate," and so on. I finally found "goat head and offal." I unfolded the bloody butcher paper, took out the head, and wrapped the offal back up, unwieldy liver slipping out of the bag until I got it all neatly packed in. Head in hand, I took it over to my counter and readied my nerves.

Laying my sharpest and most flexible knife nearly parallel to the bone, I removed most of the flesh from the skull with little fanfare. I struggled to remove the ear canal and eyeballs, attached to the brain and skull with what seemed like steel cables. I suppose eyes and ear canals shouldn't readily evacuate themselves from the skull, but sawing off tongues and tugging at eyeballs were not acts I had ever envisioned myself performing. Yet I was remarkably calm, the full weight of my actions striking me as I stood over the trash can. Or perhaps it hit me while I was scouring the kitchen, looking for just the right utensil with which to excavate the contents of the skull. It was the same sense of incredulous pride I often felt in those first few months and would feel again and again as I attempted to master skills that would have repulsed me just a year before. Now my coworkers were the only people getting nauseous as I set my tools down next to the waiting skull to search for a better implement.

I settled on a shallow metal spoon with a bent handle. Seconds later, there I stood, scooping goat brains and talking casually to customers, as if the head I held was a cantaloupe.

I began laughing uncontrollably in response to some of the appalled faces that passed my counter as I performed my task. The irony was hilarious to me. The guy with "vegan" tattooed on his neck, the guy who scoffed at a Palauan friend's traditional pig roasts and swore to never kiss a carnivore, was now not only eating meat but committing acts that most omnivores couldn't stomach. I continued chuckling to myself as I scooped and flung, scooped and flung. Staring down into the trash can at the usual pile of bones and trimmings adorned by the new addition of brains and eyes, I knew there was no going back. I had done more than cross a line. I obliterated it.

However monumental that day had been, scooping brains had nothing on the electric charge I felt the day it was finally my turn to break down a goat myself. In this early period of my butchery education, I was only starting to learn and form opinions about ethical sourcing. I knew only that the pastured goat I named Billy had come from a farm in upstate New York and that two of our regular customers had each special ordered half the goat. I did not have an opportunity to see Billy's farm, nor did I meet him while he was alive. In those days, I didn't even know visiting the farm where my animals came from was an option. It would take me many more months to gain the knowledge needed to start a group of projects that reflected my personal ethics, but working at this counter with Bryan is where I began to form those moral codes.

Billy's rose-and-ivory-marbled carcass lay in wait. With tingling ears and throbbing heart, I looked into his eyes as if I were waiting for his approval or permission, perhaps hesitant about doing this while he watched. Not until I slaughtered my first animal would I feel so tangibly and personally accountable for the life lost in order to feed us. Roughly the size of my border collie, the naked goat carcass was a humbling and sobering presence. I was a medic before entering the food world and can never resist a bit of anatomy and physiology when I break down whole animals. The horns had been sawed off, but there were two little stubs left. Studying the cilia of the ear canal and the comically crooked teeth before severance of tendons and ligaments, anatomy becomes gastronomy.

Lower on the body, I held open the cavity that once housed the goat's entrails. There, two kidneys hung by dense fatty tissue from the spine, and the liver and heart rested inside the rib cage. I placed the liver, which had been removed by the slaughterhouse, in a large bowl for offal. With two small cuts, the kidneys were free, and one more big tugging cut of the aorta and the heart was free as well. With the cavity empty of organs, I began counting vertebrae, using the side of my thumb to palpate the evenly spaced mounds of bone cushioned by bands of muscle stained deep red from the carcass being bled out.

One . . . two . . . three . . . four.

I picked up my boning knife. With slow and deliberate action, taking in every detail of the animal lying before me, I used an upright butcher's grip to pull my blade straight through until I hit the spine. A path had been prepared for my bone saw. With the rest of the body held firmly to the board with my left hand, I sawed through the spinal column and set the head aside. I positioned it so that it faced away from the rest of the body.

It did still have its eyes after all. It felt morbid to have it watching me, tongue hanging comically to one side as I parceled out the rest of its body. Reaching inside the body cavity, I counted again, making a cut between the last two ribs, up eight more, cut, and again just before the pelvis, cut. Sliced from spine to belly in three places, the carcass resembled a bear claw pastry, each primal cut nearing full amputation. The bone saw returned to aid in the secession of each primal. With each cut, I moved to successively abolish the squeamish vegetarian inside.

With the grunt work behind me, now came the act of turning those rough cuts into gorgeous rib racks, neatly tied leg and loin roast, and my favorite—lollipop chops, so named because the chop resembles the candy, with its long bare bone capped by a round of lean meat. A selection of offal, shanks, and stew meat rounded out the yield of a bit less than twenty pounds, and two very happy New Yorkers took home local goat for the first time.

This would be just the tip of the iceberg, the first of countless times that I would have the honor of following food through its many stages from source to plate. Every butcher knows the certain primal satisfaction as knives move through flesh and fat, skin and bone. The grace of this craft is as addictive as it is centering. There's a calm focus and relaxed elegance required in butchery that belies the more obvious blood and guts. The dance of power and control takes years to master, and I felt the muscle training taking root that day.

How a vegetarian of fourteen years ends up at a butcher

counter, knife in hand, is where my story spins off into the dream I continue to live each day. My mind swam with streams of problems and corresponding attempts at solutions the moment my hand touched flesh, and I've been on the trek for answers ever since. It began with Billy and continues today. Through a blog started in 2009 called "The Ethical Butcher," I shared my reflections and experiences as I learned. The family of projects that fell under this controversial "Ethical Butcher" moniker were several and varied. From educating others about the art of butchery to working as a community chef, I sought out ways to offer information and resources in a manner many have never encountered.

It was an admittedly difficult proposition, to harness these years of constant travel and new faces and perpetual metamorphosis. Where does one end the timeline? At thirty, I am yet a young chef, and butchery is a trade that takes a lifetime to master. Why am I writing this at all? Believe me, I've asked myself.

Anyone looking for a golden collection of paternalistic edicts may struggle in finding that chapter. I stood by for fourteen years, thinking my abstinence from meat and animal products was enough to change the meat industry. Coming out of that haze is when I finally started connecting the dots, when I realized that shedding the dogma that demonized meat and animal farming above all grievances was the first step to an honest commitment to changing my involvement in the food system. I decided to focus this book on those early transitions and revelations of my journey, to share the stories and faces that shaped my understanding and work of the Ethical Butcher project from its conception in 2009 to the very end of 2011. My work did not end there; this is a lifelong affair, but these words will never make it to you if I include the hyperlocal Paleocentric daily meals I've been serving to a crew of workers on a California medical marijuana farm for the past two weeks, my menus from this past summer in Montréal using pork and produce from an anarchist farm in rural Québec, or the series of community brunches produced by 718, a radical queer chef collective I cofounded with two other chefs in Brooklyn in early 2012.

For the purpose of this book, I believe it is important to lay the foundation first. I've come a long way from that morning with Billy. The series of dinners, workshops, and lectures developed over the course of Ethical Butcher projects became ways for me to engage in both casual and formal conversations about sustainability with everyone from farmers in the field to diners at the table, and they showed me endless ways of being "green."

I want to shake up this dialogue and prove there are a myriad of ways to work within and without the system. I have zero interest in telling people what and how to eat. I have astronomical interest in showing people where their food comes from, explaining government and corporate manipulation of information, and in making the "sustainability" conversation more accessible and relevant to people of all backgrounds.

A generic list of dos and don'ts is insultingly simple

when one takes a real look at the problems with our food system. Besides, aren't there enough books lining your shelves telling you what to eat?

This personal memoir through food could be summed up in two parts.

One: what I did and how I did it
Two: information to help you do it FOR YOURSELF

Like everyone else, it is through the obstacles I have faced—both in the kitchen and outside of it—that I have formed my view of the world around me. It is from this place that I hold out my offer of resolutions and observations. Each pebble and boulder in the road has chipped and polished my constitution and offered landmarks by which to write my own map. While this book will certainly spell out the conclusions I've come to thus far, it is by no means conclusive. Through my nomadic events and unique approach to the food industry, I have formed my own food philosophy, an extension of my personal code of morals and ethics, which are in direct relation to who *I* am at the core. I speak solely from my own experience. My food rules are therefore dynamic and personal and hardly informed by the latest trends or articles. I base my everyday food choices, whether for myself or for a dinner for forty, on my actual experience of everyday life. This true accountability and integrated perspective on our own behalf is the key to moving forward. No book will change this system, no green guru will whisper the answer in your ear in the grocery, and no sticker or label is always trustworthy. We each make a choice every day about the world we want to live in. It follows then that we want to look at the ways we eat with scrutiny, because what, why, and how we eat is shaping the planet and our future. Throw out the guilt trips, give up on the jargon, and look in the mirror. Real food is still out there for all of us, and it is up to all of us to take it back.

PART ONE

1

How It All Vegan

Food possesses me. I have been in its grasp since I can remember. I believe many chefs would describe themselves similarly. We don't just love food, or love to eat, or love to cook. We surrender to the limbic drive; we let food run our lives. What a life it gives in return.

My first memories are sitting in the lap of my *oma* (German for grandmother), sipping coffee from a spoon and gnawing on zwieback, a twice-toasted, faintly sweet old-school teething biscuit. My oma had moved to the States in the late 1950s after marrying an American GI. She would tell me stories of her childhood during World War II in Germany, of what she called "war food" and of school bombings. I guess since the days of Grimm, Germans have had a penchant for telling kids dark stories. She used to tell me that she started sneaking into the still-segregated barracks with her girlfriends as a teenager to catch a glimpse of the tails they were told all Black men had. She didn't find tails, not vestigial ones anyway. But she did find a husband, and she followed him first to Tennessee and then to Tacoma, Washington, a then bustling industrial port city just north of Joint Base Lewis-McChord, a very large base for both the U.S. Army and U.S. Air Force. It was on this base that I'd be born twenty years later.

My mom had my brother and I when she was quite young and never really got the hang of motherhood after she and my dad split when I was five. My oma was my world, my heroine and role model in every way. From her, I gained an early appreciation for the hard work of feeding friends and family and the joy of nourishing your loved ones. Because she had lived in the South and then within the Black community in general, her German cooking took on a soul food accent. If ever two comfort food cultures were to meet, these two are a match made in heaven—from sauerkraut and *rouladen* one night to fried chicken or gumbo the next, each beyond reproach in their heart-stopping goodness.

With a considerable German expat community to support it, a German bakery and grocery has been located in Lakewood, about halfway between the bases and Tacoma, since the late 1960s. To this day, my oma makes weekly trips there for staples. As a kid, tagging along on this trip was my favorite part of the weekend.

Divided by a lobby that leads to a French dance studio, to one side is the deli and grocery, where she'd pick up *bretzel* and *brötchen, kochkäse, lachsschinken,* and *leberwurst.* Then we'd step across the lobby into the bakery. Even now, my heart salivates the second the door swings open. Wafts of tempered sweetness and decades of filtered coffee hit my nose just as my eyes set sight on the cases of *käsekuchen,* a*pfelstrudel,* and e*rdbeertorte.* Behind the cases stand ladies who look just like my oma, with their kind eyes and firm demeanors. I swear these same ladies have worked there since the place opened. We'd usually get a few slices of *Schwarzwälder kirschtorte* and head home or run more errands, but as a kid I especially enjoyed the weekends when we had time to meet a group of her German friends there for coffee, cake, and catching up. Sitting in the café, surrounded by pleasingly faded murals of German countryside that invited me to spin imaginary tales in my mind as I was surrounded by the chatter of oma's mother tongue, I was enthralled. Every sense was engaged.

My brother and I were both used to getting a small amount of coffee with lots of milk and sugar on most mornings, but when I accompanied her on these coffee klatches, my cup was filled by the waitress and I got to dress it up myself. I even got to drink from my very own fancy porcelain cup instead of the kid-safe mugs we used at home that I felt insulted my careful hands. I always relished any gesture that made me feel more adult. Parroting, I took my time lightening my coffee to the caramel shade of my own skin, dragging my spoon back and forth slowly through the liquid before gingerly placing it on the table next to the cup, just like my oma did.

The way that room filled with people every weekend, people who were coming to get a little taste of home—that was where I first understood the importance of food and how deeply connected it is to our identity as people within a community. It wasn't just the evenings of polka music in our backyard or shared language that made us German. It was the sauerkraut and *kaffeekuchen* too.

I see food in ways that are both profound and clichéd. It is a multidimensional subject, a point of debate, a political stance, a uniting element of humanity, a tool of warfare or welfare; food is the great unifier of life. In these many dimensions of food, I find myself in constant wonderment and awe and see endless paths for work within this universe. I can get lost staring at a plate and thinking of these paths. Let's take my breakfast this morning, for instance. Fresh, local Québec blueberries, locally milled oats, yogurt, and coffee, both also locally made. Each item in this meal can be deconstructed in a myriad of ways. The blueberry is a summer berry, a gem of the season and full of nutrients and antioxidants. I could push my chef mind into gear and think of a dozen ways to use that little blue nugget. Having recently made a blueberry hot sauce, I could stretch my experiments to chutney, a BBQ sauce, an infused liquor, or cure. I could make a compote to use in a bacon cure—each a way to extrapolate different qualities of the berry's profile. On a botanical level, I could think about how the genus *Vaccinium,* as differentiated into hundreds of species of blueberry, bilberry, cranberry, and other delicious morsels of summer, is cultivated, or the medicinal properties the berries hold. I could take an anthropological approach and track down where in the world the blueberry bush originated, how it traveled to other areas of the globe, how people have influenced this migration, or how the blueberry fit into ancient diets. I could think politically about the fact that there are so many poor people who rarely eat fresh fruit like this, or how Dole just acquired blueberry operations in Mexico and how that reflects on a larger problem of a global food system and outsourcing of jobs. I could start mixing it up and think of the politics as a chef, looking at these cheaper products flooding the market, with little fruits that barely meet the bar of these pearls of indigo magic that I desire for my next menu. I can keep going, but you get the point. Every item in front of me can be dissected in the same way. The oats, the yogurt, the coffee—each is just a door to a labyrinth.

Opening my work as a chef and butcher to these many dimensions has defined my young culinary aspirations. Until that day with Billy, where all of these worlds collided, I was just working my way around the fact that I wasn't quite sure what I wanted to do with my life. I was wandering, but not aimlessly. I was just waiting for life to show me what was right. The choices I made shortly after becoming a butcher propelled my life into action. Over the years, there have been many interviews with misquotes, misconceptions, and speculations about my reasons for choosing vegetarianism nearly two decades ago and an apparent abandonment of my militant vegan moral code the second I discovered bacon. While some have been honest mistakes, many articles have been written about my meat-free past without so much as a request for verification of facts. It is important to set the record straight, as my work with the Ethical Butcher project and stance on food politics is rooted in this time in my life. However, before explaining why and how I escaped from Herbivore Island, I have to explain why and how I ended up there in the first place—and why I stayed for so long.

Dude, It Was SEATTLE in the '90s

Of course I was a vegetarian. I was twelve when I stopped eating meat. I would have a sliver of turkey on Thanksgiving to appease worried matriarchal eyes, but I surely wasn't one of those children of hippies who were raised without meat. Meat is central to both German and southern U.S. cooking. I was just another kid in the hood, feeling the pressures of early adolescence and hating the Monopoly money food stamps we used to buy food. The angst wasn't just a mom who didn't understand, it was a school that was full of fights, teachers who didn't teach and expected little of their students, and a neighborhood where wearing the color red could get you killed on the spot. I distinctly remember having a sort of awakening in seventh grade—I HAD to be different. I wanted to break away from everything around me.

In the grunge days of 1994 Seattle, everyone who was counterculture was vegetarian. It was an early stand of rebellion and individuality. "Individuality," as defined by a teenager, roughly translating to "pisses off mom" or "like the cool kids"—*cool* of course being up for further interpretation, depending on one's interests. Shock-value mantras and PETA images got a whole generation of growing children to turn down their parents' cooking and start fending for themselves in the kitchen. While many of us learned to feed ourselves actual vegetables later in life, most of the vegetarian kids in my high school ate cookies and fries for lunch.

I've never, ever thought the act of eating meat was wrong for all people at all times. I've never thought that it was unnatural or unhealthy in moderation. Meat has been a part of human diets for most of human history and is a central part to many culinary traditions. My resistance to meat eating became purely political as I learned more about the horrors of the meat industry and became more motivated to see all my actions, and those of others, in a more political context. I was more interested in a life aimed first and foremost at less impact, respectful of all life—not to be confused with protecting all life—and to moving further away from a world that I didn't see myself fitting into anyway. For many years, "vegetarian" and then "vegan" was the chosen identity of almost anyone who felt driven to live a more responsible life, and thus I committed my energy to a mindfulness about the animal products I consumed. It is changing, but one can still go to many health food stores and not find meat for sale or expect every industrial-food-is-evil media to focus on abstinence from meat instead of the reformation of government policies and the harnessing of corporate powers. It was a juvenile means of conflict resolution that offered only a partial solution.

Well, I Didn't Do It!

After graduating high school, I choose not to apply to university. I instead directed myself to a life of applied learning. Even at that young age, I saw going into debt for my education as a bad choice, especially since there wasn't anything particular I wanted to do. How many Starbucks baristas have fifty thousand dollars in loans or on their credit cards with not only no hope of repaying them but without work that makes use of the education? It is a deplorable situation. I made a choice to live a life of work that values above all direct experience, community involvement, and self-determination.

I started with a job at a progressive preschool in Seattle. This was no day care. I was working alongside published experts in the field of early childhood education at a school that is legendary for its radical approach to early learning. Working alongside these people, I was finally exposed to the language I'd needed to explore the world and find my place. Instead of solving the world's problems through my refusal of meat, I began to see all my choices as deliberate actions in what was referred to as antioppression politics. Here is where I first heard people use words like *antiracist, antibias, queer, accessibility, nonviolent communication,* and *transformative justice.* All of these words essentially meaning: "Be a normal, nice person to ALL people AND challenge a world that seeks to keep other people down due to any aspect of their identity." I was just eighteen and had been somewhat sheltered from the Northwest punk scene that spurred a lot of this work; these were words that referred to a fight that I didn't know was happening. This fight felt holistic and pure in its determination to overthrow the world as we know it. I was so ready to join in. I still find the most commonality with those who see themselves as intrinsically, diametrically opposed to the status quo.

Working with the teachers at this school, I attended my first demonstrations and felt the fire of shared rage that changes governments and is thus often quelled by police. It was also while working at this school that I began to form an understanding of how race and class intersect. I began to not only see more firmly my station in life as compared to that of the families I worked for but also to identify my own movement and transgression of class lines as a political action in and of itself. The rich don't want the poor to succeed, and despite the "rags to riches" fables they feed us to keep us chasing the carrot, this capitalist system makes sure most kids with a drug-addicted father and a teen mother don't achieve greatness. That's just fact. It was around this time that I had my most pivotal experience as relates to my class identity, the first time I realized that growing up with less money wasn't a purely financial disadvantage.

I had been dating my first girlfriend, Angela, for a few months by the time I was invited to accompany her, her family, and some close family friends on an annual trip to the Oregon coast. It was exciting enough. I had never been to the Oregon coast before, and I always loved the rare trips my family had made to Ocean Shores, a small beach town on the southern Washington coast. We weren't really the family vacation kind of people. My oma went home to Germany once a year, and my brother and I used our savings to fly to Alabama every summer to visit our dad and his family. If we had family in from Germany, we would drive up to Seattle or out to Mount Rainier. I had, however, been working a full-time job since I was sixteen, and the freedom of driving unleashed my budding wanderlust. I would take long drives on the weekends to hang out with friends I met at the underground parties I was frequenting those days. (Yes, I mean raves. Again—Seattle, 1990s.) I would take my little Suzuki Sidekick and drive for hours just to see the road and the mountains and meet people in new cities. After school, I would drive down to Titlow Beach to sit on the shores of Puget Sound or out to the Olympic rain forest for a long hike. Travel became a solitary endeavor almost as soon as I gained the ability to move independently. Seeing a family do this together seemed so foreign to me. They had been going on this annual trip since Angela was a baby, with the same two families since their oldest daughters were babies, so this trip was the tradition of three unrelated families. That added another layer of unfamiliarity. Angela and I had been dating for about six months by then, and I had met them all and got along with them just fine. So my apprehension wasn't a matter of social anxiety. I just couldn't shake the feeling that the invitation to this family vacation was an invitation to a new lifestyle.

The first night at the beach house, the families were milling about preparing the giant meal needed to feed all three families, two of which had added younger siblings to the mix in the years after the mothers met in Lamaze class. A little overwhelmed in the kitchen by the buzz of a dozen people cooking and tasting and poking fun, I stepped out onto the deck to watch the ocean. The sun was just starting to set, so I leaned in, resting my arms on the railing, and looked out across the miles of sand and cliffs surrounding us. As the sun fell, it cast a blood orange glow across the sky and sent shimmering gold across the waves. I called out to the jovial families inside to come see the show but was drowned out by the din. As I turned back to watch the blood orange fade to bluish maroon, it hit me that they weren't mesmerized because they had seen this before. I was stunned. I was bowled over not just by the beauty but by the novelty of seeing the sun set on the ocean for the very first time. They had come to this beach together for years and watched this sunset.

This was their "normal." They weren't rich; I didn't think that. But they were firmly middle class, something I thought until that point referred to my upbringing.

Right there, in that moment, meditating on the last licks of sun on the sea, I promised myself I would be like them. I wanted to have work that felt good and supported my family. I wanted to have time to take vacations with friends. I wanted to have a life stable enough where I'd have the same close friends for thirty years and raise our kids together. I wanted to be proud of more than graduating high school and staying out of the hellish hood rapture that is the U.S. prison-industrial complex. I wanted more for my life. I wanted to WANT more. For a long time, though, I wasn't sure how that happened. I used to drive around Seattle's richest neighborhood's just to imagine what it was like inside the houses, what the residents' daily lives were like. I was a nanny for several upper-middle-class families in Seattle and lived a daily reminder of where I did and did not come from. The lives of the families I worked for were so, so different from mine. Domestic workers everywhere know this irony. You basically live the life of someone with much more money, power, and privilege than yourself, but always with a firm grip on the fact that you are The Help. As I was living with these frequent comparisons, it was hard to separate wanting a better life for myself from wanting more money. Capitalism tells us they go together.

We are all trained to think there's some shortage of resources in the world—not enough food, not enough water, not enough wealth to go around. This mind-set keeps us following a trail that leads to further subjugation to the system—thinking that we need to climb the rungs of society instead smash the scaffolding holding up this burning building. There are no shortages; there are only imbalances. A 2011 report from Amnesty International stated that with more than 18.5 million foreclosed houses in the United States, banks actually own enough homes to give our country's 3.5 million homeless people a roof over their heads. Since that leaves a surplus, one could more accurately say that there are enough homes for every homeless person AND many of the millions of Americans teetering on the edge of homelessness or living in poverty. Of course, that is not a solution being offered when the banks are the ones forcing many people out of their homes in the first place. There are individuals in the world who own more wealth than entire countries. While we buy bottled tap water and fill the oceans with plastic, oil companies poison African waterways with machinery and chemicals. We bomb settlements while pointing at the building of hospitals as justification for our presence. We send in well-intentioned college kids to dig wells and take pictures of dusty, brown babies to remind us that we are "more fortunate" in our Western bubble and that these poor savages need us—without acknowledging that we are indebted to these people for the centuries of continued pillaging of natural resources, lives, and land that has resulted in a higher quality of life for a few at the cost of many. We take from the world, from the earth and its inhabitants, and then point to our small gestures of backhanded generosity with self-congratulating fake humanitarianism that simply reinforces these imbalances.

We are told that big business is good for everyone, that industrial food feeds the world, and that fossil fuels have brought us to a highly evolved life. What we must see is that big business is good only for big business. Industrial foods OVERFEED a small population of the world with just a few crops and a lot of petroleum. Destructive practices and the search for more and more fossil fuels are dragging us to ever more perilous depths.

By the time I was twenty, this farce was becoming ever clearer. I took the full plunge and went vegan as a larger statement of my anticorporate feelings. My politics had come to a place of power in my life that meant I was willing to make major shifts in order to live by them. This felt much different than going vegetarian had eight years before. I was drawing lines all over the place that were starting to etch out the person I wanted to be.

I was making myself. Veganism felt like the ultimate Fuck You to the meat industry. Not eating meat, I thought, was helping animals who were destined for the slaughterhouse, but it does nothing for the animals that live for years in the same and even worse conditions. Laying hens face a worse fate than their fryer brethren as they are kept beakless and generally immobile, seen as nothing more than egg-laying machines. Similarly, dairy cows must stay alive—barely—to produce young and lactate to keep up with the demand for cheap milk, they endure unspeakable tortures. It was a natural progression. It seemed to me that the animals who died for meat had it best and that I had to look at all the ways I could be benefiting from animal suffering from human hands.

Extending my food choices to my overall consumer lifestyle is a legacy of my veganism. As a vegan, not only does one not eat meat or animal products, but one also abstains, to varying degrees of extremes, from all animal products. This applies to everything from the obvious items like leather, fur, wool, and skins to beauty products, beeswax, some natural dyes, and more. It also means opposition to all animal testing, hunting, fishing, beekeeping, animal farming—hell, I even know vegans who are against owning pets. Going vegan felt like a distinct choice from a place of upward mobility. I could CHOOSE. I wasn't starving. I wasn't scraping by. I was CHOOSING to restrict my consumption of nutrient-dense food based solely on political principle. It felt like more of a statement about the person I was becoming than merely a lifestyle choice.

Breaking Down, Breaking Vegan

I was so into the lifestyle of veganism that I got "vegan" tattooed on my neck just after my twenty-first birthday. As any photo of me will show, I am one of those who could be described as heavily tattooed. I sport neck and hand tattoos and honestly cannot even count the total number of tattoos I have had etched into my skin over the last fifteen years. I have collected tattoos in foreign countries and friends' basements, each of these marks serving as a milestone of some pivotal point or in honor of some new stage in my life. I have tattoos for every girl I've loved, for every city I've lived in, and for every major transition. When I decided to get this particular piece done, I was twenty-one and on vacation with Angela in San Francisco. We had been vegan for more than a year, and I was ready to memorialize all the growth I was experiencing. Angela and I share an affinity for tattoos; she is still a collector herself and might be the most adorned middle school teacher you'll ever meet. With time off and vacation money to burn, it only made sense that we would both get some work done on our trip.

We both knew we wanted to get tattoos that represented our vegan lifestyle. So one sunny afternoon after walking around Golden Gate Park, we wandered into a buzzing tattoo shop off Haight Street. At this point in my tattoo collecting, I had yet to begin choosing words as the primary decor for my body, starting with the vegan tattoo and continuing today, fitting for the writer I was to become. With words and letters distributed about my entire body now, my skin could serve as the ultimate word jumble game. When we walked into the shop that day, I knew that I wanted the word *vegan*, but Angela was going for a more nuanced homage to plant life with a strawberry done in sacred heart style—complete with flames and a crown of thorns. I flipped through calligraphy and typography books while Angela went over her straw-berry savior with the tattoo artist. I finally settled on a font that used stars for all the negative spaces inside each letter. Given that the letters in *vegan*—*v, e, g, a,* and *n*— all contain negative space, this tattoo would be full of stars. For some reason, I liked that. It is now a pretty dated style, but at the time it seemed perfect. I handed the books back to the artist who would be doing my tattoo, and he set about making the stencil. A few minutes later, both Angela and I were sitting in chairs having bundles of needles drawn through our skin. I never remember the pain, but I do recall being incredibly proud to show off my tattoo that summer.

While it still strikes some as a misfortunate, youthful choice, my "vegan" tattoo is one of my favorites, surely one that is most demonstrative of my personal narrative. It tells a story about who I am and how I got here. I might not be writing this book if I hadn't gotten that tattoo. I knew I wouldn't be vegan for the rest of my life, but it felt like such a big statement about where I was in my search for the "right" way to live. It was at the beginning of a total synthesis of my lived experience and political perspective; I was making a choice to allow my politics to influence every aspect of my life. It was also an outward commitment to a set of values, a sort of public account-ability. Like having a cross or praying hands tattooed to remind yourself and others of your beliefs, having "vegan" on my body publicized my beliefs and made me a visual member of a group of like-minded people. These days, people point it out and assume that I regret getting the tattoo. However, I still wear it proudly and with very little irony, even with a dead pig draped across my shoulders. Regrets are for mistakes, and my veganism was no mistake. Going vegan made me who I am.

Just as I chose to go vegan, I chose to "break vegan," as they say, or to stop following vegan principles. I made the decision in preparation for a three-month backpacking trip across Europe that Angela and I were planning. I had heard stories from vegan friends about surviving on bread and fruit and peanut butter for weeks on end. That sounded like being fed by kindergartners for the rest of my life. I knew we'd have a better time and experience more if we were at least able to taste the wines and cheeses, eat pastries and crepes. Vegans can eat their fill in other parts of the world, but the cuisine of western Europe is fairly heavy on meat, fish, and dairy, so trying to hold vegan lines would have meant a pretty dim trip for our palates.

Opening our diets to dairy felt luxurious in its practicality, but it would also make us better houseguests. We'd be staying with my family and friends in Germany, and I didn't want to be that American guest who demands my hosts bend to my habits. I wanted to be able to accept my eighty-year-old great aunt's hospitality. In hindsight, it is still one of my greatest regrets of that trip that I turned down a plate of my favorite rolls that she had walked to town to buy simply because there were a few pieces of diced ham sprinkled on top of them.

"Ungrateful brat," Tante Hedi would have been in the right to think. I was so fully immersed in the egotistical dogma of the Church of the Righteous Herbivore that I couldn't see the ham-bedecked roll as a gesture of her love rather than a representation of my politics. Looking back, I wish I had just gone all the way and enjoyed the charcuterie (traditional cured meats) and meat-filled dishes of the ten countries we visited. If I could take it all back, I would have tasted every version of ham throughout Spain, Italy, Switzerland, and Germany and done a fair amount of research into traditional bacon curing methods. Instead, I just ate my life's allotment of pesto, gelato, and crème brûlée.

When we got back to the States, I decided to continue to make vegan lifestyle choices, as in not wearing leather, but I continued to incorporate some dairy into my diet by eating cheese and yogurt occasionally. Angela continued to swing back and forth from vegan to vegetarian, and to this day she is not a meat eater. Stubborn Capricorn. I didn't eat eggs or drink milk for another two years, still opting for soy products, but by the time I was preparing to move to New York City in late 2006, I had started to shift to the idea that eating "real" food was far better than eating "nonanimal" food. I had been having a hard time digesting soy, so I trained myself to eat eggs for the dense nutrients and quick protein they offered, and I switched from margarine to butter. I say "trained" because eggs are absolutely appalling in texture and smell if you haven't had them in years. Though I now love eggs in all forms, back then I had to plug my nose while they were cooking because the sulfuric smell made me nauseous. I liked the fact that I knew so much more about what was on my plate, even if it was not all plant derived. I don't know why it hadn't occurred to me that butter, made from cream and salt and nothing else, was worlds better in flavor and infinitely more natural than the mixture of factory-direct hydrogenated oils in the margarine tub. It was a struggle, but slowly, real foods were making their way back to my diet.

I am thankful for those vegan days, as they not only influenced my political life but were also my earliest attempts at experimental and elemental cooking. Expanding my palate and cooking style to a wider range of dishes has been instrumental in the formation of my own style of food. Through needing to be creative with unknown ingredients and opening my mind to see the bigger world of food available to me, I gained an odd manner of classifying foods that has lent itself to a very adventurous cuisine. My chef peers will understand this phenomenon, which slowly formed, where I began to relate foods to one another in very odd ways. I saw foods in intangible mental images of colors, shapes, sometimes even sounds, not just as literal, physical, individual ingredients.

Even though my style is completely ingredient driven, it is this tool that allows me to separate the physical item in front of me from its form and transform it in unexpected ways. A potato is just a potato, but I can replace it in almost any traditional potato recipe with an apple or cassava or turnip and get a rise out of a group of bored diners. In building those flavors, I'll move from something I sense as round, like brown sugar; dampening, like molasses; or loud, like lime juice or chili pepper. If something is too spicy, too sharp and loud, I know I can meet with it something that is equally pointy, like a lot of citrus or tomato, or soften its blow with fruit juice or honey. Giving up animal products didn't mean I was going to give up on food that tastes good. Cooking as a vegan made me concentrate on building flavors. Even though I use that skill to cook to-die-for meat nowadays, it is a talent fully based in my vegan cooking mind. I continued to rely on these skills as my diet expanded and, more importantly, as I began to work in the food industry upon my move to the Big Apple.

2

Gnawing Questions and Biting Answers

It made sense that when I landed in New York, ready to start a new life, I ended up looking for work that would finally let me grow into the person I wanted to be that night on the Oregon coast. I wanted work that wanted all of me. So much work in this world is about compartmentalizing. Workers are just that, workers. They aren't friends or collaborators or conspirators, just easily replaced cogs. I had escaped that feeling over the last few years while working as a medic in Portland, but I'd need a new shtick in New York.

I got a job in a wine store on Union Square. As I stocked bottles on my first day, a lightbulb clicked on in my head, right in time with the first clink of bottles: I realized I *belonged* here. I knew from that day forward, I would work only in food. I had always enjoyed food culture but for some reason had never considered a career in the field.

Now, the fire had been lit. Over the next year and a half, I set out on a culinary circuit training of sorts. Within a month, I was researching wines for staff tastings and jumping at the chance to help a customer choose a wine. After just a few months though, I was ready to try something else. Wine was interesting but a little too stuffy for me. I wanted to get out of the dusty stockroom, but I absolutely loved helping customers with pairings and readily absorbed the information about growing processes, *terroir*, and varietals while discovering that I had quite a sensitive palate. My next stop made use of these new skills, as I became the cheesemonger at a brand-new shop in the Carroll Gardens neighborhood of Brooklyn. The chef/owner of this only-a-little-pretentious prepared foods/cheese shop was an accomplished, hotheaded, CIA-trained kid who had just opened his solo venture a few months before hiring me.

Jeremy Wachalter was the total textbook chef. He made people cry. He cursed at customers and canceled vending accounts based on the tiniest errors. I remember one day when a bakery screwed up our order, giving us too few of one kind of roll and too many of another. He was on the phone with the bakery in a flash, screaming, "Don't ever send us your shitty bread again." Yes, in the food biz, a mistake like getting the wrong amount of rolls can mean going out to buy something retail or a really annoying day of explaining to customers why their favorite sandwich looks different today, but as a reaction to a first offense, it was overboard. Morale is everything in the kitchen. The chef that uses verbal abuse to get results is teaching to the lowest common denominator. Fear is not respect or admiration. Your whole crew sees how you work; customers see how you work. As chef, your every move in the kitchen becomes a series of norms that set the culture of the entire space. We had new hires walk out after their first hour on the job or disappear after a lunch break. Jeremy even had me lie to a client, telling a bride who was waiting for him to deliver some catered dishes that he had been in a horrible car accident, simply because he was stuck in traffic. As far as I could tell, he didn't respect anyone and didn't feel bad about it. I was personally rarely on the receiving end of his bad behavior, however. In the months I was there, I took over buying in order to save relationships and smooth things over with a few vendors who swore they would never deliver to him again.

This assholery is entrenched in kitchen culture, so none of this implies that Jeremy was a bad chef. I learned from him how to create high-concept comfort food. Jeremy leaned heavily on his Jewish background and classic French training. He made everything in-house in a very small kitchen and did it all very well. Keeping with Brooklyn's deli tradition, beef stews and rabbit braises, roasted vegetables, rotisserie chicken, and other thoughtful dishes were sold by the pound out of cold cases. The store provided a face and a little cushion for the cash cow: high-end catering. Jeremy kept things simple and straightforward. He was able to elevate his plates by using fresh, local ingredients and high-quality imported goods. As the cheesemonger and buyer, I bought, stored, and cared for the cheeses and kept the rest of the store and kitchen stocked. I did not work in the kitchen next to Jeremy and am thankful that I got to learn from him by watching, eavesdropping from the other side of the pass, and tasting. I also took my first step toward stepping off the Veg Train while working for Chef Jeremy. It was my job to handle the rotisserie chickens we sold, which often needed to be cut into quarters before customers took them home. When you aren't used to even touching meat, just the sensory experience can be unnerving. To tell the truth, I *still* hate cutting up chicken, which is slippery and mucous covered when raw. Sliding the impaled hens off the spit back then, it was a daily struggle to not betray my disgust as I cut and packaged the glistening, crispy little hens for Brooklyn's elite.

While I had camaraderie with Andrea, the manager of the store and his other valuable peacekeeper, we couldn't hold on to even one employee for more than a month or two because of his behavior. We eventually stopped trying to hire people who could stand his fire and instead, we poured ourselves into keeping his boat afloat. Between the harsh toke of life in NYC high-end catering during the holiday season, rich and usually rude customers, and a boss who screamed at anything that moved, by the time we made it to January 2009, I was done. I left that post and stationed myself at a restaurant in DUMBO where a bunch of new friends worked. There, under Chef Laura Taylor, I picked up an appreciation for attention to detail and respect for the natural, inherent qualities of ingredients. Laura craned over a sink for hours every single day, soaking and sorting baby greens for her impeccably perfect salads. Every individual leaf had to be perfect, not ripped or torn or browning in the least. I found it strange that she chose salad greens of all the things on the menu to obsess over, but I now understand that drive for perfection in the even the smallest detail. For a few months, I worked the grill on the line at lunch, cooking burgers and steaks. I learned tricks for cooking burgers to temperature by touch and learned how to clean and grill fish, how to clean a beef tenderloin and marinate flank steak, all new skills for me since I hadn't eaten meat in over a decade. You'd be surprised how many vegetarian chefs there are who don't restrict themselves to vegetarian restaurants. I thought I would be one of those lifelong vegetarian chefs who expertly prepare dishes they will never taste, but I was wrong.

After a few months, I decided to keep my learning moving forward and to look around for a second job. I came across an ad for a new gourmet foods shop that had just opened close to my house. I recalled Jeremy having consulted on a similar project, so I figured I'd test my food world connections for the first time and see about their cheesemonger position. A couple weeks later, I was waiting outside of The Greene Grape Provisions in Fort Greene on a June morning, waiting for the most important job interview of my life. Not that I was aware of it at the time. It turns out the owners and Jeremy had already parted ways, but they were enticed by the fact that I had worked at his shop. Needless to say, I was hired, but not to age cheeses. I was told that the current cheesemonger would be around for a few more weeks and that in the meantime the butcher and fish counters needed help for the summer. I was unsure, but the work looked interesting and the pay was better than what I was getting in the kitchen. This job appeared to present an unexpected solution to both my immediate and conscious search for a better-paying job and my more subtle and lasting search for my place in the food world.

On my first day, I met Bryan Mayer. Now Josh Applestone's (of Fleisher's fame) right-hand man, Bryan is the picture-perfect ex-bassist rock star/new school butcher. He's got the tattoos and a salty Brooklyn charm that endears him to anyone who doesn't get fed up with it. Bryan had gone from a life of touring with his band and working for an ad agency to running the counter at the shop in just the few months since the store had opened. Bryan and I connected immediately, and the brotherly competition that we'd develop pushed us both to become the butchers we are today. Over the next year, we learned together, taught each other, and eventually challenged each other to become more educated about the trade we had both just taken on. As we both uncovered ever-sobering information about the state of the food industry, there were days when we felt more defeated than accomplished. We actually used to sit over our whiskeys after cutting all day and lament the scarcity of truly sustainable beef and the demise of the oceans due to bad fishery practices. A strange conversation to overhear between two heavily tattooed dudes at the bar, I'm sure.

This relationship is like that shared by many others in this trade and was one of the reasons I started to fall for butchery. I refer to Bryan Mayer as my "mentor" butcher out of respect for this bond. Bryan was not yet the skilled butcher he is today and taught me in a much more fraternal manner than one would expect to see in an apprenticeship. I found butchery to be a dynamic and diverse trade that beckoned me forth to expand and explore everything I had ever enjoyed or taken an interest in. It is hard, bloody, physical work that requires not just heavy lifting but wrestling with dead weight for hours on end. At a densely packed five foot six and 145 pounds, I have now become more than accustomed to hoisting pigs that outweigh me over my shoulder. Our work looks brutish, but a brute could never master this art form. The degree of control and the balance of strength and skill needed in this trade call for someone who is smart and tough. You have to know when to ease up and when to push harder. You have to be good at creating mental maps and possess a certain amount of kinesthetic intelligence— meaning you must be able to sense where all your fingers are at any given moment. Knives and hands are seen as complementary tools, so we find ourselves doing exactly what all chefs are trained to avoid: cutting in the blind and quickly alternating knife and fingers in the same task, as both are required in the employ of breaking cuts down. We must be dancers to find the rhythm that will keep all appendages intact. Miss a beat, find a filleted fingertip.

I was pulled into the challenge of mastering this trade I had demonized for so long. The old medic in me was intrigued by the opportunity to dissect animals on a regular basis in a way that used both science and art. Relying on anatomy, you learn to sculpt an object that is at once aesthetically pleasing and flavorful. Diet, exercise, stress hormones, and other biological aspects of the animal's life show up in the characteristics of the resulting meat. Traditions of butchery and charcuterie are more varied than one can imagine, and a single cut can be steeped in history. All of these nebulous ideas combine into something so tangible to become the very definition of "real." Two weeks into the job and I was hooked. I had fallen for the forbidden fruit of butchering meat but had yet to taste it. I am too deliberate in my decision making. Just because I was interested in the craft of butchery, didn't mean I was ready to eat a seventy-two-ounce steak.

I had to mull it over. In addition to wanting to learn more about butchery, I had little gnawing questions of my own. What was my vegetarianism really doing? What was the end goal? If it was corporate greed and inhumane treatment of animals I was against, was abstaining from meat the best way to fight? Once scrutinized, what began as a genuine movement concerned for animal welfare was starting to feel like a status symbol, a badge of honor for self-control and temperance. Day after day, I went to work thinking I was ready to take the plunge, but I held back each time I thought of taking a piece of meat home as Bryan had been encouraging me to do. "C'mon, B," he'd say, waving a small piece of steak in the air as an invitation. It wasn't about peer pressure or giving in to the magnetic powers of meat; it was about understanding my medium. Now that I've trained a few vegetarian butchers, I see why he was prodding me.

As a butcher, you are a trusted element of your customer's life. You must become a walking index of cooking techniques cross-referenced by species and cut so you can anticipate what they'll want for dinner and how they'll want to cook it. Even though I was practicing the tactile skills of cutting, there was a huge disconnect between me, my customers, and the food I was selling to them. I was learning more about my new trade, and part of what I was learning was that I had to be an expert. After working in wine and cheese, two food fields where unending knowledge is revered, I felt like an utter novice standing behind that counter fumbling for answers to questions from customers. "I want to grill some steaks tonight. Which ones should I get?"

Weeks into my new job, I knew how each steak was cut and where on the animal it originated, but I had no clue as to its flavor or texture. I'd invariably guess based on what I saw other customers buying and say something like, "Well, a lot of people enjoy London broil," which I later discovered to be maybe the worst cut to suggest for the grill. I have always prided myself on being a bit of a know-it-all, so this shoulder-shrugging, shot-in-the-dark manner of giving culinary advice began to wear on me quickly. I loathe ineptitude and could only imagine what the more knowledgeable customers were thinking as I stood there peddling my wares.

I began to deconstruct my reasons for staying on the veg side of the line. Even in the days of my militant veganism, I was incensed not by the normal and healthy consumption of meat or the inherent loss of life but by the greedy and harmful corporations I saw as the sole beneficiaries of a system that abused animals, polluted the environment, and produced disgusting, diseased meat. This anticorporate sentiment was a strong thread in the fabric of the '90s Seattle social consciousness I grew up around and was mirrored in the desire to fight all forms of oppression that had come to color all realms of my life.

From what I ate to what I wore to how I got around to how I treated others, I had long been on a mission to continually raise the bar for my personal behavior higher than what I had been led to believe was acceptable. It was becoming a dilemma. I knew I'd start eating meat soon, but I still hadn't made it to the point where I felt justified in breaking the only real rules I had ever held myself to. At twenty-six, I had been vegetarian for literally half of my life. Not eating meat was as much a part of my identity as the thrifted duds that defined my personal style. If I started eating meat, would I next be wearing sweatshop clothes from The Gap? I had to find the rationale that made becoming an omnivore an action that advanced my politics, not one that compromised them. After weeks of daily internal debate, I found the bridge I had been searching for.

It seems at times that I found that answer literally INSIDE of the meat I was working with. It was a normal day of wrangling the inner vegan, that petulant whining voice making me doubt what my new work was teaching me every day. Standing at my counter that day, I was deep in reflective thought while breaking down a beef rib section. The task requires the separation of the large loin muscle from the rib cage. Picture a giant book with many pages. The cover of the book is the rib cage, with the spine of the book representing the spine of the steer. Inside the cover, or rib cage, is a whole lot of meat—boneless rib eye to be exact. Removing that valuable meat from its frame is a tricky task that calls for alternating knife and fingers in quick succession. Starting from the top of the ribs, one slides the knife in between the meat and bones, and through hundreds of small, quick cuts, the hunk of marbled meat slowly releases itself from the cage. The usual technique is to free one side all the way to the spine and then turn the rib around and work from the opposite edge. This results in an effect much like holding that book upside down by its cover, with the meat hanging from the spine and waiting for the last few emancipatory swipes of the knife. A typical beef rib section is about sixteen inches tall, meaning that at the apex of this task, a butcher's entire forearm and hand are inside the cage, deepening and widening the space between rib and loin. It was at this very point that the light flicked on.

The more I learned about meat, the more I realized that I had been fighting something I didn't even understand and using tools that weren't working. I was not somehow a better person or less implicated in the suffering of other living beings by abstaining from meat. The meat industry is still kicking, and my vegetarianism hadn't changed that; nor had it taught me anything about the appropriate living conditions of animals. Meat was murder—that I accepted—but I couldn't tell you how a cow should actually be treated. I knew nothing of what went into caring for these animals. I still get into arguments with vegans and vegetarians who have never stepped foot on a farm. I feel that this class of herbivores is a direct result of the chasm between farm and table. We don't know where our food comes from, so it follows that especially those who purposely distance themselves will possess even less knowledge about the chain of action from farm to table. They've disengaged and dismissed the issue based on the idea that the problem lies only on the backs of those who eat meat. Such a defeatist position is nothing but privileged apathy. We Veg Folk were focusing our energy on the wrong target. You don't fight by turning your back on your opponent and plugging your ears. You train; you learn his moves. You look him dead in the eye, tell him his days are numbered, and then you pummel him. Jeez, haven't any vegetarians seen an action movie?

Hands still deep inside this cavity, I felt the connection to this animal, to its life and death, to the farmer who raised it and to the customer who would eat it. If I was the one choosing the farms and cutting the meat, if I was the one explaining to customers why I was choosing one farm over another or why we wouldn't be carrying a product anymore, I was the one with the power to change the entire system. It was about being engaged in building the world I wanted to see. It was no longer enough to wash my hands of the problem. Once I saw this role as a way to truly effect change, I was compelled to become an active part of the solution. While I am quick to say I am not antiherbivore, that day I certainly became PRO-omnivore. Like flashes of fluorescent buzz lighting up in a long dark room, I felt a tangible brightness take over me. In that moment, I was exhilarated by my position as butcher. Now I was ready for a fight.

All of this occurred as I made those last few cuts along the spine. I let the meat fall down onto my cutting board. I set the now empty rib cage aside, sliced off a thin piece of meat, and handed the sliver of flesh to the cook next to me. Knowing how momentous this relay was, she asked if I was sure. "Yeah," I said, "do it."

Moments later, she returned with a strip of cooked beef on a little napkin. I took the juicy little strip and popped it in my mouth.

When you haven't eaten flesh for over a decade, the

texture of meat as you chew it is a completely foreign sensation. I should say that over the months I had been contemplating eating meat; I had been taking the tiniest bites of fish to prepare myself. I was still under the common conception that fish was not meat and was a more responsible choice—I'd later find out that I was sorely mistaken. But at the time I felt that fish was sort of like a primer for whenever I did decide to eat meat— even if it was years down the road. While I contemplated the toothiness of the steak, the strong flavors filling my mouth took me by surprise. I finished chewing, with my accomplice coworker watching my face as I went from alarm and surprise to the meaty glow I've come to recognize in many who have broken their vegetarian rules at my events. Having said nothing up until that point, I looked at her and simply said, "I'm back."

I was more than just "back"—I was reborn. Now incited to a new way of waging battle against an old foe, I set out to learn everything I could about butchery. Over the next few months, I would learn and perfect many more butchery skills, and I eventually took over the fish counter that adjoined our meat station. Now Bryan and I were on a roll. He pushed the meat counter toward the goals we had both come to understand as important in running our shop responsibly. Those goals were whole animal butchery and local sourcing. As he worked on that front, I overhauled our fish buying program and sought to become the first fish counter in the city to offer a completely sustainable selection of fish. Due to the fact that so many types of seafood are fraught with sustain-ability issues, this meant a much more limited selection than our customers were used to seeing. Even more than working the meat counter, this was my first major foray into consumer education.

I started with nixing every species in the case that I knew to be unsustainable for one reason or another, but I was told by the shop owners that the farmed salmon and wild tuna were off-limits because they were customer favorites and their sales floated a large portion of the profits for the fish counter. With that sole restriction, I bulked up the case with shellfish and the few species I found to be responsible choices. To explain to customers why they would no longer find swordfish or flounder in the case, I printed out large posters depicting every wild capture method as well as the most common fish farming methods. I hung a large sign that described what fish were in season at any given time. People don't know much about meat sustainability, but they know even less about the practices of the fish industry. If I could point to a photo of the long lines that often snag seabirds and turtles in addition to a target species, or explain to someone that trawling the seafloor is like plowing a field six times a season, most of my customers understood why I was making a change. Of course, some simply responded, "But, I LIKE cod!" to which I'd invariably respond with something like, "I didn't say cod doesn't taste good. I said it's bad for the fish and the ocean, so we won't be carry-ing it in the store anymore."

We humans have a regrettable knack for making everything about ourselves.

Between fielding questions like "Why don't you have certified organic wild salmon?" and "How many breasts does one chicken have?" I became aware of the fact that it wasn't just ex-vegetarians who needed to learn how to eat meat and fish responsibly. If I was in a position to dispel misunderstandings and educate consumers on more responsible choices, it seemed that I was duty bound to do so. So I did what any self-respecting, opinionated loudmouth does nowadays. I started a blog—and I gave it the name "The Ethical Butcher."

I started the blog with the goal of helping people understand their choices when it comes to buying and eating meat. Though I did indeed want to dismantle the pedestal of moral superiority many vegetarians cling to, I did not want to give people an excuse to eat meat without guilt. I wanted to centralize meat eating in the discussion of sustainable food. The ways that I would do this with my blog changed greatly over time. I began with the idea of listing grocery stores and restaurants that sold responsibly sourced animal products. The vision was for the blog to become a reference for people who were looking for a good spot to grub down on some well-raised meats. I also felt that ex-vegetarians like myself were everywhere, and I wanted to connect our collective experiences in the blog as encouragement to others who were wrestling with their herbivore identities. For many of us, dropping the veg label was like leaving a church. People lose friends over this, and I felt that if those soon-to-be ex-vegetarians had the stories of others in their minds, they may feel more empowered to make their own choices. I also found that many ex-vegetarians shared a similar desire to swing to the far extreme by not only eating meat but reveling in it. Not all of them became butchers, but some of us did. Even those who don't make a career of meat take on a new appreciation for it. As people who at one time in their lives made decisions based on the treatment of animals, they are not eating meat without taking accountability for the loss of life involved. They want to hunt and fish for themselves; they want to learn how to tan hides and carve bones. They eat hearts and kidneys and caribou and rabbit when lifelong meat eaters stand in horror at the mention of those words. We understand that a whole, sentient being has died for our meal, and we solemnly accept that sacrifice. Nothing gets my blood boiling more than someone who eats meat but shudders if I refer to the chicken as something that lived. Many who have never stopped eating meat pretend chickens don't have faces, cows are made of burgers, and fish are somehow less evolved than their land-based counterparts. Ex-vegetarians never make this mistake. We know what we are doing. We take responsibility for it. That aspect alone was a reason to pull together a resource for ex-vegetarians. With our higher standards for animal welfare and wholehearted acknowledgment of the death necessary to bring our favorite meal to life, WE are the ones who will change this system.

I invited my new readers to submit essays about their transition from vegetarian to omnivore, with the only criteria for submission being that the writer had to have been a complete vegetarian or vegan (NO pescatarians) for more than three years. I received several essays. My favorite was written by Canadian poet and blogger, Andreae Prozesky, and sums up the entire spectrum from young vegetarian to adult vegan to meat lover:

My Life without Meat—by Andreae Prozesky

I spent most of my youth as a vegetarian. When I was a child, I was just picky; I would eat chicken and turkey and fish ("fish," in Newfoundland, meaning cod, and only cod), but, as I would explain, "no quadrupeds." In any form. I didn't eat hot dogs (making me a great annoyance at birthday parties), I didn't eat hamburgers, I didn't eat local delights like Maple Leaf Vienna Sausages (a lunchtime staple at my school) or fried bologna sandwiches (a lunchtime staple at my house). I didn't eat sausages or bacon or anything else that would once have trod the earth on four feet.

Aside from some sort of delicate sensibility, I have no explanation for this aberrant behavior. My mother admits that she was a vegetarian for some time before she had me, but it was the seventies, and so were all the hippies. One theory is that once, as a toddler, I ate cubed ham with such gluttonous abandon that I made myself ill and could never eat pink meat again.

Another factor might have been that my father had a small hobby farm where he raised chickens and ducks and geese, some of which he slaughtered by sticking their heads through what was called "the killing cone" before lopping them off. In retrospect, I can guarantee that the lives and deaths of these animals were as humane as could be, and I would pay a great deal of money to be able to go out and buy chickens who had been given the same treatment, but at the time I found the whole affair appalling.

When I was maybe twelve I began my serious attempts at vegetarianism, which lasted right up until my early adulthood. I lived primarily on canned kidney beans and whole wheat toast, peanut butter and jam sandwiches, and instant Alfredo-style noodles. My mother, though sympathetic (and an excellent cook), was a working mother of two, short on cash and time. She did her best to balance my diet for me, making cheese sauce for me to eat with my French fries, and introducing me to a world of curries—channa masala and samosas, primarily, those most entry-level of Indian foods.

When I was a teenager, all my friends became vegetarians, too. I ran with a crew of activists and do-gooders, and I could often be found hanging out at the Peace Centre or the Youth for Social Justice office, writing letters for Amnesty International. We organized rallies against ecologically destructive municipal planning and for freedom in East Timor, against domestic violence and for fair trade. Against Nestle and for better resources for refugees. Against oil dependency and for bike paths. Whatever the leftist cause was, we supported it, sometimes blindly, but always enthusiastically.

Part of the leftist cause package was environmentalism, and part of that was animal welfare. How could any of us believe in a better world and still continue to enslave hens and cows and bees? How could we eat candy with insect-based shellac? How could we wear leather boots and still hold our heads high? This last one was a very difficult one indeed in the age of Doc Marten. Somehow we rationalized it, probably because we were all sixteen and hadn't paid for our own boots. The awful things our parents did with their money would be on their karmic records, not ours.

I didn't convert to veganism right away. I didn't want to have to explain myself to my parents. St. John's, Newfoundland, had one health food store at that time, and it was expensive. Also, I hated tofu. When I got to university in Montreal, though, I was the boss of my own kitchen—at least, my third of it—and I decided to give the vegan thing a go. I'm still not entirely sure of the reasons, but I think it was mostly just to prove to myself that I could. It wasn't about fitting in; I was miles away from the vegetarian crowd back home, and I hadn't made any new friends in Montreal yet. Maybe it was about self-control. I'm not sure, but I went into it whole-heartedly.

It was at this time that I really began to learn to cook, and I'm glad I did it while I was living under dietary restrictions, even if those restrictions were self-imposed and arbitrary. I think this is what makes me such a versatile and intuitive and creative person in the kitchen. When you don't have the standard array of ingredients to choose from, you're forced to think of foods as more elemental. I think I'm a better cook for never having seen dinner as a matter of meat and two veg.

I was also eating things like dairy-free spreadable margarine called "Canoleo." There were a lot of other things going on at the time that could have made me feel crappy and chubby, like being in university and reading a million books at a time under fluorescent lights. My diet, though, was certainly a large part of it. Despite my best efforts, veganism did not agree with me. After two years as a vegan, and of driving my friends and family quietly insane, I decided to go back.

I started eating dairy and eggs again, and that helped. But I was also sneaking off to a local greasy burger chain where only Francophones ate and where I would be sure never to run into people I knew. I would order chicken burgers—no fries, nothing to drink—and I would inhale them. I also would pick up a half dozen of the creamiest, most obscene pastries I could find at any given bakery (not difficult in Montréal), and I would take the most meandering alleyway route home, stuffing them in my face until the box was empty. Clearly my relationship with food was a little skewed.

A couple things happened to help me reevaluate my diet, and to eat meat and dairy and eggs again without guilt. The first of these was a trip to Germany and Poland with my friend Anna. Anna is Polish, and we stayed with her family in different parts of Poland for a month.

When Anna and I first got to her family's homestead in the southern part of the country, her relatives had prepared all kinds of meaty dishes. These were people with little money, but they had a vegetable garden, some chickens, and they had access to local meat of all description. Her people were woodsmen, hunters and such, and they understood all about the relationship between people and the animals they eat. If I knew then what I know now about food, if I had felt the same way that I do today, I would have been inquiring as to where I could get my hands on some boar sausages, but no. Anna tried to explain to her family that I was a vegetarian—if there is a Polish word for vegetarian, nobody at the table knew what it was. "In Canada," she explained, "Andreae doesn't eat meat."

"Oh," Anna's doting aunt replied, with a look of surprised pity. "She must be very poor." And with that, I was given the largest piece of meat at every meal, despite my objections. No matter how I felt about eating animals at the time, it would have been unforgivably rude to have turned the meal down. So I ate it. A lot of it. And it was quite delicious.

I returned to Montreal after my trip to Europe, not quite a jolly omnivore, but one who could eat rotisserie chicken from the Portuguese shops without hiding behind a dumpster to do it. At least now I had

*an explanation for my lapsed veganism: I had been to
Europe, I had eaten the delicious, delicious cheeses and
meats, and I wasn't looking back. But I still wasn't
eating those troublesome quadrupeds.*

*After I finished my university stint, I moved up
north. Way up north to Yellowknife, in the Northwest
Territories. Think diamond mines and grizzled prospec-
tors. Up there, hunting is a way of life (as it is, in fact,
here, but I had rejected that as part of my leftist package
of values). Big game hunters from the U.S. and Europe
fly in, all decked in camouflage, toting enormous rifles,
to be taken up in airplanes in order to shoot caribou,
buffalo, muskoxen. The aboriginal people and estab-
lished White folks who make up the population make
much less of a show of it, and their freezers and pan-
tries are stocked with wild meat. Everyone also wears
slippers made of smoke-tanned moose or caribou hide,
which smells exactly like lapsang souchong tea. It's a
marvelous place.*

*I wasn't a rabid carnivore up there, either, for the
first little while. I ate caribou burgers (often over-
barbecued to a hockey-puck-like dryness, due to the
fact that caribou meat is very, very lean). I ate fish,
pulled daily from Great Slave Lake and the other lakes
around it. I worked at a restaurant that served grilled
caribou medallions with wild berry sauce. Once, and
only once, I tried muskox jerky. And whale blubber.*

*Then, one evening, I went to a party with some
friends, where one of the hosts had roasted caribou*

*tenderloin in a crust of rosemary and hot chili flakes.
He had started it out at blast-furnace hotness, and then
turned the oven down to almost nothing while the meat
cooked, gently and juicily. I still think about that dish
all the time. It was absolutely phenomenal.*

*About that time, I got pregnant with a child who,
there was no doubt, would turn out to be a meat-eater.
I was so hungry for meat that no moose or caribou
would have been safe walking past my rustic—and yet
adorable—backwoods shack. At the music festival that
summer, I hung out with all the other pregnant ladies
at the so-called "cultural area" (but jokingly referred
to as "the calving ground") where people cooked all
manner of meat over two giant fire pits. Whitefish?
Jackfish? Burbot? Yes, please. Caribou, bison, elk, and
bighorn ram flown in by someone's cousin in Alberta?
Bring it on!*

*When I left Yellowknife and returned to the more
genteel ways of Montreal, I was too poor to eat meat
for quite a while. And, since it had all been farmed
and not shot unawares on the barren tundra, it didn't
taste quite right when I did have it. But I got used to
the blandness of factory meat after a while. When I
moved back to St. John's a year and a half later, I was
eating a pretty standard diet of vegetables, grains, and
the occasional roast chicken. My daughter was happy
with that, and so was I.*

*Then I fell in love with an unabashed meat-lover.
Raised in a family where meat formed the focal point*

of every meal aside from macaroni and cheese, my husband can't wrap his head around vegetarianism at all. He likes his steaks bloody and his turkey dinner submerged in gravy. He enjoys a good pot of moose stew. He makes a mean hamburger.

After two years in the House of Meats, I'm an omnivore in earnest. I'll be thinking about meal plans for the week (the sort of thing you do when you're a housewife and mother of two), and I'll say, "You know what I could really go for? A ham." Me! Eating ham! Truth be told, pork was the final frontier. I know that, for many ex-vegetarians, bacon is the gateway meat, but not me. It wasn't until last year that I ate ham for the first time. I've only been eating pork chops and stuffed tenderloin and what have you for a few months, and I've still never picked up a piece of bacon and eaten it, although I cook with it all the time.

All this meat-friendliness makes feeding a family much easier. Children, and husbands with unnaturally high metabolisms, need a lot of fuel. Pretty much everything we eat is cooked from scratch, and, let me tell you; it's a lot easier to throw a piece of meat into the oven than is it to assemble an adequately nutritious vegetarian casserole. My daughter can't eat gluten, which is the backbone of almost all quick-fix vegetarian meals (and, given my suspicion of processed foods, I'd take a high-end, all-beef frankfurter over a scary wheat-and-soy-product veggie-dog any day of the week). I don't mean to sound like an advert for the meat producers of Canada, but I will say this: Meat makes my day easier.

Unfortunately, where I live, the accessibility of humanely and sustainably raised meat is limited. As I said before, many people hunt here, and I can usually track down a moose roast or some stew meat from someone over the course of the year. There is a lamb farm close by, and I am in the process of finding out how I can get involved with them—a friend had mentioned the possibility of going halves on a lamb this spring, and I'm all over that idea. I know that there is someone raising ducks in a community about forty minutes away, but I haven't been able to make contact with them yet. There is one grocery store that sells local meat, but it's just outside of town and I don't have access to a car, so there's another impediment there.

I have two local-meat goals for the next year. First, I want to develop a taste for rabbit. It's one game food that's easily found—if you can borrow a car and head out on the highway in the fall, chances are you'll find someone at the side of the road selling hares by the brace. People in Europe go nuts over wild rabbit, and I'm lucky to be able to get it. I just have to get over my emotional prejudices against it. You know, cute little bunnies and all. And skinned rabbits look like cats, and that freaks me out just a bit.

I also plan to eat seal meat for the first time. The north Atlantic seal harvest is probably one of the most controversial animal hunts in the world, but the controversy is unfounded; sealers hunt conscientiously and efficiently. The perception that the seal hunt is conducted entirely for the sake of vanity (read: fur coats) is a very lucrative one cooked up by the animal-rights crowd. Seal meat is eaten in Newfoundland and Labrador, and while it's not a mainstream food in the cities, it's considered a delicacy by many, especially people of the older generation. Seal flipper pie is the most common use, and flipper dinners are held every spring by church groups as fundraising events. Flipper pie has become a rallying point, a symbol for local sensibilities in the face of international interference. It's our slow food and this year, for the first time, I'm having my in-laws take me out for a nice flipper supper.

If I had to name a favorite meat-based recipe, it might be the simplest: a nice, rare steak, grilled over an open flame. In the woods, by someone you love. With some decent red wine and potatoes cooked in the embers. What lentil loaf could possibly beat that?

I never did find out how the seal pie went over, but Andreae's essay perfectly describes the journey so many of us have traveled. In addition to these more political and philosophical reasons for eating meat, I found as I grew in my culinary skills that working with meat was the missing key to being fully immersed in the world of food. It is undeniable how deeply entrenched meat and meat products are in many culinary traditions. Meat is sacred.

In learning to treat this gift with respect, I feel that I have found a way to honor the animals that have died to produce food. I feel so connected to life when I serve meat. So much energy travels from farm to plate. In this transfer of energy, we tap into a relationship to the world that has existed for millennia. From the sun that feeds the grasses and roots to the animal that ingests them, we take in the light of the world. From the hardworking hands of the farmer who takes months or even years to bring an animal to slaughter, to the capable hands of the butcher who uses years of knowledge to skillfully transform carcass to cuts, to the talented heart of the chef who takes hours, days, months, and years to elevate that energy to penultimate levels, meat connects everyone from farm to table. Given that unbroken chain, it only makes sense that we should all want to improve the flow of that life-giving energy. Our current system does not honor this obvious fact. Instead, the industry skips steps and cuts corners and pushes production to unsustainable extremes.

Meat is not meant to be eaten several times a day, every day. It is meant to be a hard-won prize. Whether that prize is won through the hunt or through working with natural cycles and living creatures to produce healthy, edible livestock, meat is a treasured nutrient. We have this despicable meat industry precisely because we don't respect that fact. On average, Americans eat over two hundred pounds of meat a year, per person. Considering that most adults only need about fifty grams of protein A DAY, this figure is astronomical, and remember, that's two hundred pounds *on average*, meaning many people eat much more. They do not do so because they have to or because it is healthy, but just because they can. We have convoluted financial stability and a comfortable lifestyle with frequent meat consumption. This cycle of overproduction and overconsumption has been a self-perpetuating ticket to the food crisis we are in today.

The problems of overproduction follow the same pattern in the food industry as that of many other industries. By making a stand on this issue, we begin to fight a system that is feeding us to death. We must see more clearly and have a collective recall of more than a few days. People can't scramble to buy the latest gadget every six months and then stand aghast when it is revealed that the technology company might be providing less than living wages and humane working conditions for the people making those products. The same system that keeps pigs in barred cages to feed a sick market and forces diseased meat into the world puts people behind bars to work for free. The same system that clear-cuts in the Amazon for beef production starts wars in the Middle East for control over fossil fuels. Is it a coincidence that we live in a society that has no qualms with pumping animals full of medications or altering the genes of tomatoes yet denies working people lifesaving treatments and access to preventative care? I don't think so.

When meat is a part of the discussion, somehow seemingly disparate topics start to overlap. Environmentalism, animal welfare, human rights, economics on both a local and global scale, corporate corruption, and flaccid governance all come together on the plate. Just like that blueberry from my breakfast, the steak or pork chop carries the weight of the world straight to the table.

When we start to see these worlds collide, our disparate fights also gain strength and momentum. The system moves on as it does because those in power have so far largely succeeded in keeping us from rising up in unison. It is a boon to all revolutionaries and activists of history that we are all able choose the front for which we feel best suited, but imagine if we had the ability to coordinate our attacks. What would happen if tree-hugging squatters in Oregon organized with prison abolitionists in Philly and teachers' unions in Chicago? One hell of a war, that's what. We see it in fits and spurts now. The Occupy movement of 2011 harnessed that power for a few months, when millions of people from all walks of life, with a variety of grievances, filled the streets of countless cities demanding change. The unchecked capitalist system we live under gains from the fences we put up between our own respective movements. Our separation is their validation. We must see this as an affront to the unmet potential we have for bringing about a world that is truly healthy, happy, and secure for all. Even with the world's wealth concentrated in the bloody clutches of just a few people, those red-handed bandits have us convinced that this is in our best interest. The saddest and most defeating part is that we have continued to believe them.

Once I saw meat in a political context, I saw a way to make my entire life about political action through art and community. Understanding how much more could be accomplished if the same ideals, dedication, and passion that fired my vegetarianism could be used to guide choices in meat consumption and the way that fits into the greater food system, I began to feel that I could truly change the world around me. I dove in, looking for ways to bring my vision to fruition. The strong network of experiences, analysis, skills, and projects that I now call the Ethical Butcher began to sprout in the fullness of that day a few years ago with Billy. They continued to widen as I moved from working behind the retail counter and attempted to turn my blog into a business upon my return to the West Coast in the summer of 2009. It is there that I was able to advance my work to a new stage of development.

3

Isn't That an Oxymoron?

Pigs and I are fated friends. I became a butcher before I ate meat. This is my calling. This elegant craft is my destiny. I am the grandson of Alabama hog farmers raised by my German grandmother—what else am I supposed to do? But, you might be thinking, why on earth did I choose such a name?

Butchery is craft, a skill, one that takes years of practice to master. Ethics are morals and philosophy in action. Since morals are inherently personal, the words *ethical* and *butcher* are only mutually exclusive if YOU think they are. Nothing I can do will make the physical act of butchering itself more or less ethical. Butchery is what occurs *at* the block, knives in hand. The ethics come in on either side of the block. It is still butchery whether I get the animal from a sunny green pasture or a dismal feedlot. The ethics guide how to choose the animal, how to make use of it, and how to relate to consumers in representing the meat, the farms, and the farmers. One who dresses and sells meat can indeed do so in a manner of or relating to a set of moral principles. There is no absolute incongruence, no oxymoron.

I chose "The Ethical Butcher" as the title for a piece I wrote for a zine put out by Brooklyn Anarchists of Color in 2008. I was aiming for the gut, not the brain. I was only a few months into my life in meat, just forming some vision around the circles of my experience that were beginning to meld. When I decided to hop on the blog train, I tested out several titles. I had heard of a "Healthy Butcher" and a "Gourmet Butcher," and "Berlin the Butcher" was nixed because it is too close to "the Berlin Butcher," a nightmare of a post–World War I Berlin butcher-serial killer who sold the chopped flesh of his victims as beef and pork.

With that unfortunate coincidence in mind, it only made sense to go with the title that had spun the frazzled layers of ideas into the beginnings of a cohesive set of practices that would help me feel like I was doing the "right" thing as a butcher and chef. I began to use "The Ethical Butcher" title to pull together the group of projects I did between 2009 and early 2012. I chose this name not because I, personally, am THE ethical butcher but because I wanted to present myself as the ETHICAL butcher. The title refers to my practice of dissecting ideas about the meat industry and reforming perceptions about food. As my blog gained attention, I found myself learning to defend the title publicly even as I defined and built my platform. Over the years, I have had to grow into and along with that choice of title. I have had to define and refine my use of these words in juxtaposition and have shaped and reformed my connection to it over that time.

Slowly, I began to build the philosophy that came to govern my work. The main tenets of all the Ethical Butcher projects served as the reasons why I shifted focus from a capitalist business venture to a community chef model. They explain why I start every single menu at the market—in every city, at every time of year—and why I don't charge $120 a ticket for my events. While I have certainly shunned all forms of dogmatism when it comes to my food choices, there are most assuredly a few lines in the sand that I have imposed on myself and my work.

Each of these five principles can be stretched into an entire conversation on its own. I will first give a short explanation as to how each principle affects my daily work and how each piece fits into the overall EB philosophy before examining each point in depth and through practical application. I've arranged the tenets in a somewhat chronological order, with the founding ideals moving into a few later additions that came along as the Ethical Butcher projects took on a life of their own. These were lessons informed either by my personal experiences on the road or by those of friends in the field. I spent all my travel days in search of collaboration with chefs, farmers, and other butchers who held themselves to many of these same standards in their work in the food world.

Main Tenets of the Ethical Butcher

1. Seek Out the Most Responsibly Produced Sources Available

The original driving force behind the Ethical Butcher was simple: Find good meat. For me, that meant local meat from responsible farmers. I wanted animals that had eaten the food that evolution has prepared them to eat, not corn and soy. I wanted animals that had unfettered access to free space and social time. I wanted to work with farmers who respected their animals and the earth. It all seemed like it would be a tall order to fill. However, I quickly found that buying good meat wasn't the difficult part. Get whole animals from local farms and use them in events; this feat was impossibly easy. I was able to find farms nearby with just a few phone calls and e-mails, visit farms to meet farmers and see living (and dying) conditions, and buy the meat directly from them. People were happy, and it was all very simple. It was actually everything else that proved hard to source responsibly.

One of the few hard rules I made was "No Seafood"— or rather, *very* little and *very few* types of seafood. Aside from animal products, produce was an issue. Conventional produce is sprayed with chemicals or coated in waxes, which have obvious human and environmental impacts, and produce can be quite expensive, depending on where you live, especially "organic" produce.

In addition to these more traditional notions of "sustainability," those that refer specifically to growing/production methods, I soon began to see myself drawing lines on other elements relating to food.

I learned that achieving this simple task of finding good food, not just good meat, often means striking a balance between several of these scales of measure, and nearly every event presents a new set of variables to consider. There were economic and environmental considerations, especially in relation to the transportation of food—not only on the production side but on mine as well. I couldn't beat Big Oil if I needed several trips in a gas guzzler to produce an event or build menus around imported products. I also carried an oddly neurotic hippie guilt about my frequent air travel. I was, and continue to be, heavily invested in displacing my carbon footprint by biking or using transit to get around—or at the very least restricting my driving to the day of an event. As a more frequent consumer, I generally take my economic engagement much more seriously. You may think nothing of buying a small piece of blue fin, but if I put it on a menu, I'll need twenty-five pounds, meaning I'd be adding substantially to the demand for this threatened species if I used it regularly.

For years, I had stores I wouldn't shop at and brands I wouldn't buy, but running a food business has intensified that reality. For any given event, I may be plugging money into several local businesses, from grocery stores to kitchen supply stores, or deciding whether to purchase imported goods from countries with varying relevance to my political life. My boycott list has expanded exponentially since starting the Ethical Butcher project.

As I will explain in great detail in later chapters, the "best" choice changes with the season, location, logistics of transportation, and a host of other factors. Now that the rules weren't boiled down to meat versus nonmeat, I found that there was no static formula to follow unequivocally in order to feel that I was always getting the most oppression-free food. However, leading my work with this goal in mind, I slowly began to further refine my vision in order to create new ways of walking in the food world.

2. Choose Natural, Traditional, and Local Over All

I have my own checklist of what constitutes healthy food and have, from my vegan days, a sort of natural inclination toward accounting for each individual ingredient I use in my cooking to ensure a wide variety of nutrients in every meal. This meant lots of local in-season vegetables and a strong focus on traditional methods of food preparation. I will predictably always take the option that has changed the least from its original form or is closest to its original state. In a word, I prefer *whole* foods— whole fruits and vegetables, whole grains, whole milk, whole animals—foods that have been processed as little as possible. Why would someone think for one second that some mechanically manufactured, soy-textured, vegetable-protein "chicken" is healthier and more environmentally responsible than a chicken raised on open pastures, eating bugs and worms? REAL food is always the answer. If you couldn't make it at home, it is likely to be something you should not eat. As they say, only cook food a grandmother would recognize.

Just like Grandma, to ensure the quality and integrity of my food, I make almost everything from scratch. I don't just butcher the meat I serve. I cure, pickle, jam, and bake. I make my own hot sauces and ice creams and infused liquors. Cooking from scratch like this gives ultimate control over quality and keeps budgets way down. One can certainly afford to eat healthy, flavorful foods if priority is given to time finding and cooking quality ingredients. Anything I don't make from scratch myself—with the exception of spices, salts, and other pantry items—I buy directly from a small, local producer. This not only gives me more access to information about how the item was produced but gives me an opportunity to support and build a network among like-minded food folks. My produce comes from farms or local cooperative grocers. If I need wine, I'll go with a local winery. When I need bread, it comes from skilled local bakers, like a favorite worker-owned bakery in San Francisco or one in Harlem owned and run by immigrant women who make traditional breads from their respective cultures that I feel lucky to patronize. Sourcing locally looks a little different when I need items that just don't grow locally, like coffee or chocolate. When I lived in Portland, mecca of coffee roasters, I formed direct relationships with a few shop owners. This allowed me to buy coffee that was coming directly from well-paid coffee growers in far-flung locations but was roasted just blocks away from my house. Ethically sourced cacao is now used by many small chocolatiers, and every city I have worked in has producers of local jam, honey, beer, distilled spirits, wine, cheese, and many other items. It is an honorable experience to taste these local products everywhere I go.

I have a very strict no soy and no corn byproducts policy. You see, when it comes down to it, where many point fingers at the meat industry for its hand in the sad state of our food system, it is actually corn, soy, and precious petroleum that are propping up this broken machine. Cutting these three items from the table automatically removes many harmful processed foods from one's diet. Lowering the consumption of petroleum products is a matter of reducing the distance my food has to travel to get to me, as in buying locally. Since many food dyes are petroleum based, avoiding processed foods with artificial coloring is also a given. Avoiding factory-farmed, corn-fed meat, as well as trying to source only pastured animals and not using processed foods at all, made keeping away from corn byproducts pretty doable. My abstaining from soy went fairly unnoticed while I was doing meat-centered dinners the first couple of years, but when I started offering full-spectrum menus (vegan to meat) last year, the no soy rule became more of a talking point. Now my meals are a bounty of plant-based foods, with small portions of rich, decadent meat.

After years as a vegetarian who relied on soy for protein, I developed a severe sensitivity to eating it. Hearing this same experience from other ex-vegetarians, I decided it was important to offer soy-free vegetarian dishes as a gesture of support for those on the other side of the fence. The soybean is one of the most common genetically modified organism (GMO) foods on the market. In fact, it is one of the GMO foods many other processed foods are based on and is present in the vast majority of commercially available foods. Since the Food and Drug Administration refuses to compel corporations to label these foods, the best way to reduce exposure to GMOs is to avoid soy and corn byproducts as much as possible. I couldn't very well serve GMO tofu sammies next to my slow-cured, chemical-free, GMO-free handmade bacon.

3. Provide Accessible Community-Focused Elevated Cuisine

Access to food, and especially food culture, has deep roots in classism and racism. Food has also served historically as a tool of oppression. North American bison were killed not only for the massive profit of colonizers but to starve the First Nations peoples throughout the expansive plains of North America into submission. J. Edgar Hoover considered the Black Panthers' food program one of the greatest threats to national security precisely because they were filling the poor with nutritious food and energy to fight another day, as well as information that empowered them to see the world around them more clearly.

I found food culture in general to be boring, stagnate, and bound to tradition in a way that keeps large-scale innovation from taking place. Most of the food world is just another prism of the dizzying capitalist kaleidoscope. Even after removing the issue of working with corrupt government, I had to address the role food service has in the delineations of class in our culture. I didn't just have to find new ways to get good food on the plate but new ways to serve plates too. I became mindful about the type of people I attracted to events, moving over the years away from rooms of foodies. I have deliberately shaped my events to draw in a range of people, and I price them so that all kinds of people can attend and interact. I refuse to work for the moneyed class, seeing that as merely reinforcing centuries of servitude by generations of talented Black cooks kept hidden in the kitchens of the rich. By serving my food to the kind of audiences I feel connected to, I feel that I am circumventing the mechanisms in place that assign people to their rightful castes. Food is comfort and healing, and *my* food is for *my* communities. And that feels just as revolutionary as any other step in a world where those outside the mainstream are invited in and allowed to prosper only if they are willing to be consumed by the mainstream.

I have come to develop a style of cuisine that follows my politics. I send out plates that are steeped in tradition and full of intention but adventurous and unexpected. I am resourceful and flexible in my planning and strive to surprise myself with every menu. My food doesn't talk down to my diners, and I don't cook to the lowest standards. I entice people into unfamiliar territory with food that seems like something your mom used to make, even if it is something you've never seen before. By focusing on feeding and educating my own communities, rather than simply pandering to the green elite with my dinners, I am making a stand, because EVERYONE deserves good food.

4. Support Fair Labor and Environmental Practices

Our society is built on theft. I am a descendant of a stolen people; we live on stolen land, and we consume stolen labor and resources as a matter of fact. Everything that composes this Western postcolonial, postindustrial world was built on the backs and bodies of others. In addition to this inescapably sad truth, it is also true that some of the most lasting atrocities committed in these centuries of "advancement" have been related to food and labor. Early American "Thanksgiving" feasts were dedicated to celebrating massacres of First Nations peoples. As clearing indigenous peoples from their lands freed up space for colonies to grow, this mass extermination-as-eviction was seen as cause for riotous feasting. One such feast occurred the day after seven hundred Pequot people were killed, another featured their decapitated heads as soccer balls in the streets of what is now small-town Connecticut, and yet another saw the head of the chief of the Wampanoag being impaled atop a pole in Plymouth, Massachusetts—where it remained for twenty-four years. Millions of lives were traded for sugar for HUNDREDS of years through the Atlantic triangular slave trade. That does not include the many millions of lost lives considered lost cargo, thrown from ships to lighten the load or lost through sickness and injury on the long journey.

Just as bodies and lives were traded for profit back then, our postcolonial industrial world depends on this same lack of reciprocity. Migrant workers risk their lives to cross borders full of both civilians and officials bent on their demise only to reach working conditions that barely recognize their humanity and to be demonized for "stealing" those jobs from "real" Americans. Chain grocers boast cheap prices on food but fail to mention that they don't pay their workers a living wage or provide health care. Considering the many layers of issues presented by poverty, a system that provides cheap food while keeping people poor is essentially a guarantee that social imbalances continue.

Corporations are responsible for global environmental destruction, which naturally impacts both the people and animals that live on those damaged lands. Greenpeace reported in 2009 that clear-cutting for grass-fed beef was the leading cause of deforestation in the Brazilian

Amazon, with more than 214,000 square miles occupied by cattle ranches. According to the Center for International Forestry Research, the portion of Europe's meat imports from Brazil rose from 40 to 74 percent between 1990 and 2001. Since many indigenous peoples live in the Amazon and rely on it for their lives, deforestation at the behest of Western markets is just a repetition of the pattern of pillaging that has plagued the world's indigenous peoples for centuries.

Aside from threatening animal species and populations that call the Amazon home, disputes between corporations and activists across the globe have been known to become violent and even fatal. A recent report by Global Witness, an organization that works to uncover links between environmental exploitation and human rights abuses, gives a sobering reminder of the cost of standing up to the big guys. It states that 711 activists and journalists have been killed over the last ten years in the course of defending or investigating land and forest rights, with more than one hundred of those murders occurring in 2011. Since 80 percent of Brazil's beef production is based in the Amazon and much of that meat is bound for foreign markets, these figures are alarmingly relevant to the discussion of responsible meat eating. But these figures don't stop at beef. Bananas, grapes, coffee, and many other foods produced globally carry very similar stories. Dole Food Company was mired in a lawsuit for years after Nicaraguan field workers organized to fight the company after years of toiling under showers of the pesticide dibromochloropropane, or *DBCP*, in Dole's banana fields. Though the nematicide was banned in the United States in 1977 due to its causing sterility in males and ease of exposure, and despite the fact that rival companies Chiquita and Del Monte stopped using the dangerous substance, Dole publicly continued to use the product in large amounts on its plantations throughout Latin America until 1982. Since DBCP can be absorbed through the skin or inhaled, anyone who has seen the photos and film footage of workers trudging through puddles of the toxin would come to the conclusion that the sterility of the men working those fields was at least partially due to their contact with the product. However, it took years for successive waves of litigants to get the company to finally settle for an undisclosed amount.

I believe it is my role as an activist and chef to fight corporate food and to try my hardest to limit the ways in which my work and my commerce support these corporations. Of course, legally I am not allowed to point to the decades of complaints, allegations, and violations involving these giant companies—not if I want to live outside a courtroom, that is. Because of food libel laws, our judicial system's protective shroud around the food industry, anything seen as "disparaging" to a particular food product is grounds for a lawsuit. Remember when Oprah Winfrey was sued by Big Beef for $12 million just for saying she wouldn't eat burgers after the mad cow scare? Well, I'm not Oprah, and I couldn't afford one day in court let alone fight the hawks that guard the food industry. What I can do is source meat and produce as responsibly as I can, so that I am never left to ConAgra products from a grocery store where employees aren't provided with benefits, steak that came at the demise of the Amazon, or fruit that was picked by an eight-year-old. Otherwise, I would only be perpetuating the system that I aim to destroy. This is a gap that many fail to cross and one that vegetarianism failed miserably at addressing.

Humans make your food, not animals. From the slaughterhouse workers who are forced to process THOUSANDS of animals a day under deplorable conditions to the workers picking berries in the fields of central California, humans are being abused in the interest of providing cheap food. Just as I seek to find solutions to issues of sustainability that pertain to the environment and animal welfare, I *must* seek solutions to issues of sustainability as they relate to the people who make our food.

The veg set has been so successful in making people aware of the plight of animals in the industry that the discussion has been skewed to the extent that people will vote to support animal rights before they will jump to the defense of their neighbors. This imbalance played out in the 2008 elections, when California voters chose to ban veal crates for calves and battery cages for laying hens and then stripped the right to marry away from same-sex couples. If you do not see the problem there, you prove my point. To stand in arrogant ignorance of the suffering of fellow humans in your defense of animals, to fight for the liberation and humane treatment of animals without first demanding the liberation and humane treatment of people, is inexcusable.

Most relevant to my daily work is an entire restaurant and food-industry labor force made up of undocumented and therefore unprotected, often poorly treated, workers. Aside from the long hours for little pay, mainstream kitchen culture is generally a White Boys Club built upon a staunch structure of patriarchy that is unapologetic in its acceptance of misogyny, classism, and racism. From the dishwasher being paid five dollars an hour to the maître d' or host—invariably someone who can at the very least *pass* for White and upper middle class but is nonetheless obliged to placate patrons in hopes of a five-dollar tip for graciousness—fine dining is a textbook exercise of capitalist elitism at its best. Servers in some restaurants never leave with less than three hundred dollars in tips after a shift, while the kitchen crew, the people who *make* the food, are lucky if they work in a restaurant where servers share tips with the kitchen. In spots like this, a crew of six might be lucky to get eight bucks a piece after a slammed night of one hundred plates or more. A little disheartening in an environment where verbal abuse is normalized and hazing is commonplace.

Chefs are notoriously bad at taking care of themselves, substance abuse issues are widespread, and many of us put in fifty-to-eighty hour weeks dazzling diners and then survive on takeout, toast, and scraps from work. I wanted to be dedicated to fair treatment of all as well as self-care.

I made a promise to myself way back that I wouldn't hire anyone until I had health insurance. You can imagine— I'm still flying solo. Not yet at a point where I can hire people and compensate them well, I turn my scrutiny on those with whom I collaborate and, to the degree I am able, to the farmers and producers I source through.

Starting every menu item from scratch means having more control over not only the quality of ingredients I use but also the working conditions that go into my menus. For my cooking, there are brands I avoid like the plague, there are brands I use with restraint, and there are brands I love. With this rule, I assume all are guilty until proven otherwise. The realities of capitalism mean that companies are more likely to be cutting corners somewhere to achieve maximum success. By most every measure, cutting corners and skipping steps is often in the interest of the final profit. Streamlined efficiency, heightened productivity, uniform consistency—these are the signs of progress and expansion that business minds look for. Reaching these goals often comes at the cost of employee wages and safe working conditions. I am not a labor analyst, and I don't have time to research every single producer of every product I use. I don't travel to olive groves to assure that workers who make the olive oil I use are being treated fairly. For the most part, I stay in the know by working directly with small producers as well as other small business owners as much as I can. Many of these producers are entrepreneurs or family businesses. If someone I work with has employees, I want to know they are treated with respect and are as well compensated as the business owner can afford. I have found cooperative and worker-owned grocers and farmer's markets to be more than sufficient for my needs and have no use for big box stores. I specifically avoid several large grocery chains, even "natural" or "organic" chains, as well as food corporations due to labor issues. If I hear negative news about a corporation or store, I'm usually ready to jump ship without question.

5. Support and Develop Radical Food Justice Practices

We all know who is responsible for this state of affairs. It is all too predictable, yet we are mystically lulled into a state of helpless complacency. We are not pushing hard enough. Until we get real and get angry and DEMAND change, this system will continue. We have to stop turning a blind eye and start to turn our backs on this whole upside-down world. Make no mistake, the only reason there is a need to distinguish between "good" or "real" food and the crap that fills our grocery stores is because the USDA and FDA are completely dedicated to enabling and emboldening the food industry and its destructive practices. The industry has us referring to genetically altered, poison-laden products as normal or "conventional" and using purchased language, in the form of a government stamp—"ORGANIC"—that distances real and traditional foods from their more pure origins and falsely positions unnatural foods as the trusted option.

Crafty devils.

The buck passes from consumer to farmer to corporation and government and lands firmly at its final destination: capitalist greed. I am not interested in settling for an alternative food system that operates in a green corner of our industrial world. For one, most "green" companies are owned and operated by the same big companies they seem to be in competition with. The irresponsible activities in the food industry are directly related to similarly irresponsible activities in the oil industry, the banking industry, and the legislative bodies supposedly regulating them. Why are deformed, breast-heavy chickens raised on subsidized corn and forced to grow so quickly that they can't support their own weight? Why are some slaughterhouses killing as many as four hundred steer an hour? Why did Dole rain down a deluge of banned toxins on its fields and workers for decades? Why are BP and the government telling us that seafood in the Gulf of Mexico wasn't affected by the 2010 Deepwater Horizon spill?

With our present methods of production, one would think these practices are in place to provide food for the masses. A noble supposition, but incorrect. The solitary reason for this gross imbalance? Ever-increasing profits, logically.

Since all of the disgusting, unhealthy, dangerous conditions in the food industry exist under the supervision of the very entities charged with keeping our food system safe, the only way to distance oneself from these practices fully is to actively work AGAINST those governing entities. For my part, I am vehemently against cooperating with the governing bodies charged with our food safety.

Early on in the course of the Ethical Butcher, after a few months of thinking I wanted to open a store, I quickly saw that I'd be much more fulfilled working with larger concepts and chose to pursue my goals through community events instead of a commercial presence. That decision took the crooks out of my circle for good. I couldn't, I can't, I don't, and I will not work directly with the USDA or FDA. It doesn't matter to me whether these government agencies are too bloated with ex-food-industry blood suckers to act in the public interest or just too weak to fight against the industry to actually protect our food system. They don't do their job, so I don't pad their payroll.

სი სი სი

Each of my three main projects worked to define, practice, challenge, and expand these five principles. Each project had its own goals and methodology and gave me the opportunity to test a new idea or grow into a new stage of development in my work.

Heritage Breed Supper Club:

December 2009 to November 2010

Portland, Oregon; Brooklyn, New York; Covington, Kentucky;
Potter Valley and San Francisco, California

The Heritage Breed Supper Club was what started it all. By May of 2009, I was gearing up to move back west. "The Ethical Butcher" blog was running well, and I was gaining a little attention with the perspective being presented. I had done my first giant bacon cure, testing out over a dozen flavors on friends of friends in Brooklyn. I felt like I was onto something in trying to move the exploration of these ideas out of cyberspace and into reality. I didn't want to just blog about meat and food as a butcher in a shop. I wanted to slow down and dig deeper. Moving home was my opportunity to do just that.

Portland's reputation for incubating small businesses attracted me. My goal at that time was to start a local heritage pork bacon business. I thought I'd sell first at the farmer's market and eventually in stores. I set about making a list of every farm on every site I could find that fit the list of what I was looking for: heritage breed, local, humanely raised, and nice, fat bellies for bacon. Since I'd be getting a full pig for my first round of bellies, I thought a dinner party with the rest of the pig would be fun. So I tapped a friend at a local hipster hotel and booked the ballroom. From there, I began a year-long project of whole animal dinners in several cities. These dinners almost always had the farmers who raised the meat present as honored guests, something I felt was very important to connect diners to their meals. HBSC dinners were formulaic: Choose a farm. Visit the farm and schedule a carcass pickup closer to the event date. Take photos. Write a blog post. Plan and promote the event. Days or weeks later, pick up the animal. Break down the animal and cook a four- to six-course meal for a private party of twenty-five to fifty guests. Introduce the farmer to the guests. Serve the meal. Plan the next event. Repeat.

The goals with HBSC were to:

1. Draw attention to heritage breeds and the concept of conservation by consumption.
2. Challenge myself as a chef to create a meal using one whole animal.
3. Raise awareness of the issues small farmers face and familiarize the community with local farmers, not by speaking for them but by inviting the community to share a meal with them and hear their stories firsthand.

Not only did this project teach me more about sourcing well-raised animals and give me more transformative experiences than words can express, but I was also able to pick up on the trends of local foods in several cities concurrently. I've seen a lot of places only from the perspective of a food shopper and can more easily name a farmer's market in any given city than a museum.

Priced from $120 for a six-course dinner on a Northern California ranch, complete with a takeaway bag of raw cuts of pastured meats as well as a tour of the ranch, to about thirty-five to fifty dollars for a four- or five-course meal of local lamb, pork, or poultry, HBSC events were most assuredly more affordable than comparable events. However, pricing accessibly didn't become a priority until later, when I closed the project in style with a party in the same venue where I had held my very first dinner the year before. That night, Portlanders paid just twenty dollars for an extravagant party featuring a film installation showing one of the farms I sourced through and a photography show with prints of images from the year of HBSC farm visits—showing everything from sunbathing heifers to a pig mid-evisceration. While diners took all this in, tables overflowed with dishes made from sixteen whole animals—local lamb, duck, chicken, rabbit, and pork—while a DJ spun dance music and a photographer snapped photos. This multidimensional aspect would become integral to my events as I moved on from these larger productions to more intimate meals with my next two projects.

The Bacon Gospel:
March 2009 to July 2011

Brooklyn, New York; Portland, Oregon; Tacoma, Washington; San Francisco, California; Covington, Kentucky

Where HBSC was the brainy elder of the family, the Bacon Gospel was the baton-twirling, attention-hungry middle child. The Gospel got all kinds of attention very quickly because it dealt with everyone's favorite meat: bacon.

The goals of this project were to:

1. Draw attention to heritage breeds of pork using a familiar and beloved food prepared in new ways.
2. Use media attention on bacon to bring up issues of sustainability as related to pork farming and the meat industry.
3. Create and serve more than one hundred flavors of bacon, developing an entirely unique method of bacon curing.
4. Use this dramatically different bacon in dishes as a star meat, not as garnish. One menu item that came out of this project and still slays crowds: GRILLED BACON STEAKS.

Unlike the HBSC, which had a definite formula, the Gospel was much more free flowing and flexible. Throughout the course of the project, I ran everything from bacon flights to curing lessons to a monthly bacon club with home delivery and massive custom-order campaigns that had me buried in ninety pounds of slabs on more than one occasion. Just as each bacon flavor boasts a snarky moniker, each city's installment had a hokey title. There was Bacon for the Queen City (Cincinnati), Bacon for the Sound (Seattle), Bacon for the Bay (San Francisco), and, most popular, BCN/PDX, a play on the airport code of Portland, Oregon.

While varied in format, every installment of this project featured local heritage breed pork cured in five different flavors, often grouped by a theme inspired by the season, the location, or the ingredients. Events were always centered on communal indulgence. Groups of flavors were arranged and served in the style typical of a flight of wine, with flavor profiles presented in an amplifying fashion, with light proceeding to dark as the flight continued. This format gave me endless room for layers of expansion and creativity between thematic concepts, flavors of bacon cures, and final dishes. From a love-inspired round of Valentine's Day flavors to a meal in appreciation of the artisanal producers of Portland featuring five flavors using local coffee and distilled spirits, I was able to put my heart into each installment. With events like a cookie-themed after-hours tasting in my aunt's cookie factory and events with DJ buddies, this project also allowed me to share work with loved ones and gave me some of my most prized memories among the many events I've produced over the years. As my traveling increased, it grew harder and harder to work curing into my schedule, and

I decided to put a hold on the Gospel in the summer of 2011. The blowout bash for this project was a two-part celebration, with an installment in both Portland and San Francisco. Each featured five flavors of bacon, including one BCN/PDX club favorite chosen from the crew of bacon-loving subscribers who had tried over thirty flavors collectively in their year of membership, presented in thirteen dishes ranging from savory to sweet. I still teach bacon curing classes, cure bacon for use on my menus, and add to my list of flavors—which stands at 122 currently.

The Farm & Table Project:

April 2011 to Present

Portland, Oregon; Olympia and Seattle, Washington; San Francisco, California; Brooklyn and Manhattan, New York

This project took the best of the first two and combined them in a way that made work much more sustainable for me. It was also this project that honed my culinary skills in ways the first two never did. Through these private home dinners done in cities with very different food cultures, I really started to see myself as a chef, and as such I started to carve out my niche in cuisine. My food began to name itself: local, seasonal, ingredient-driven, elevated American comfort food layered with Latin and Southeast Asian flavors.

The goals of the Farm & Table Project were to:

1. Take my events and discussions from a macro- to a microcommunity level by moving away from large gatherings in public spaces toward intimate dinners in private homes.
2. Provide ultimate accessibility to intentionally prepared foods. Even if priced accessibly, food events still wrap good food in a package to set be aside for a special occasion. By booking birthday party BBQs, friend-filled brunches, and romantic meals for couples on a weekly basis, I was putting myself and my food in a much more approachable position.

3. Form more direct and lasting relationships
   with diners. Both the Bacon Gospel and the
   Heritage Breed Supper Club were about putting
   the spotlight on farmers. After a very full year
   and a half of that focus, I was ready to invest
   more in the people who had been attending
   all these events. I wanted to open the lines of
   communication and open my kitchen.
4. Break down class lines in access to "luxury" by
   providing the usually exorbitantly priced service
   of an in-home private chef for about the price
   of a meal in a casual restaurant, about thirty
   dollars a person.
5. Show the ease of access to local foods and
   the culinary superiority of seasonal foods by
   creating personalized menus for every single
   client, sourced exclusively at local markets.

With Farm & Table, I fully subjected myself to the
whims of nature by becoming even more seriously dedicated to local, seasonal sourcing. I learned to see the
relationships between flavors and textures and gained
confidence in going to the market with open eyes instead
of the tunnel vision of a prepared list that allows for little
variation through the seasons. Creativity and resourcefulness are integral traits in a chef or home cook who leads
a more sustainable existence.

I so enjoyed challenging myself with the task of design-
ing new menus frequently, sometimes several a day, that
in over eighty private dinners, I have never repeated a

menu. With dozens of meals, each consisting of three to six courses, there are literally hundreds of dishes I have made for one special meal and will never make again. My favorite part of these meals is standing in the kitchen alone, listening to the contented silence of a nearby room full of diners, taking in the stillness dented only by the sound of utensils scraping plates and nearly inappropriate *Oooh, my GAWD*s.

The people I have worked with in this project have ranged from groups of twentysomething Portland eco-fashion designers passing joints around the table during my second course and radical queer performance artists who made their menu wishes in solely conceptual terms, to retired farmers who were just interested in food that tastes of memories and young Battery Park professionals who will surely become my arch nemeses in twenty years if their careers go according to plan.

∽ ∽ ∽

Every one of these projects has been an attempt to prioritize one reality of the market over another. Through whole animal events, in-home dinners, flashy fancy bacon, teaching butchery, and curing skills, I came to discover my definition of "responsible/ethical/sustainable" engagement in our food system, one that operates as far outside of the status quo as possible. The field test was more of a proving ground, but I came through it an expert in renegade chef tactics. From this place I share some of my observations and personal food rules. This is not an attempt to say I've found the answers but an invitation to all to start asking questions for themselves.

The point of these Ethical Butcher projects was not to open a restaurant or butcher shop; it wasn't to raise armies of ex-vegetarians against their herbivore enemies. The Ethical Butcher started with questions about the meat industry and led me through a winding path to a very singular existence in the culinary world. The farmers I meet in California are not unlike those I meet in Ohio, but each farmer is a unique character in possession of the keys to being able to feed us. They are the gatekeepers. Serving as a bridge between farmer and consumer as both butcher and chef is a responsibility and a privilege. I am selfish. I have to do everything on either side of the cutting stage. I want to get my hands on every step in the process from farm to table. Owning a butcher shop or restaurant would surely give me some measure of this community involvement and thrill of risk, but my attention span would have me looking for a whole new field of work in a few years. By producing nomadic events that tear down the walls between chef and butcher, farmer and consumer, I also cause the walls guarding good, safe, nutritious food to crumble. Many assume that these roving dinner parties must be my stepping stone to bigger commercial presence, but the truth is: This is it. This is my magic spell and my political action.

Connecting the circles of our food system and helping people understand where their food comes from is a duty all chefs and butchers carry. I do not do this work so that more people will eat meat or for people to feel better about meat eating. Though the Ethical Butcher projects started out on the premise that there are ethical ways to eat meat, as I learned more about the food system from the inside, I quickly came to see that it takes work to eat *anything* ethically—and even more work to feed ten, one hundred, or one thousand people with the same ethics.

In my personal life, I never became a heavy meat eater. Instead of spotlighting the meat dishes, I began investing just as much energy in creating a menu that would be indulgent for everyone from gluten-free vegans to meat 'n' potatoes stalwarts. I got to lean back into all the vegetarian recipes I'd perfected over my fourteen years on Team Veg. I felt this more accurately reflected my support for everyone being able to make their own choices. Holding events where no one was left with "rabbit food" meant full groups of friends could attend together, and events began to attract more than finger-on-the-pulse foodie types. To serve "ethically" sourced food in a setting where I was pandering only to those with the means to attend expensive dinners was just as anathema to my principles as serving plates of industrial meat.

Chefs and butchers, as a workforce in the industry, MUST change this system from the inside. We must all consider ourselves food activists as much as we are artists working an edible medium. It is the duty of those of us in the kitchen to push this conversation to the next level. We can't sit back and let sociology professors and vegan journalists do the work only we are capable of doing. We can't keep propping up a system that bends us over the rails time and time again.

I have been endlessly fascinated and humbled by the brave actions of other chefs and butchers, as well as by farmers who strive to live up to their desire to provide the world with real, good, honest food. Through learning from many of these people and experimenting with my own approach, I have finally found a radically new way to work against the system that is distinctly personal and allows my politics to follow a clear and unobstructed path from farm to kitchen to plate.

4

From Farm to Table and Back Again

I found my way to writing about food and food politics through the need to translate and share my experiences in the blog. I came to food politics through a fusing of my out-of-kitchen and in-the-kitchen worlds. I realized how much more effective it is to be principled in the way I engaged the meat and food industry. I could layer food justice work into the anti-oppression work that defines my worldview—not in theory but IN PRACTICE every single day. Not only that, but in a way that would connect people to their food system and their communities and bring true excitement and wonder back to the table. It is one thing to pontificate over the woes of the meat industry from a café or office, or even after a tour of some horrible USDA-certified centralized animal feeding operation (CAFO). It is quite another to be on a ranch deep in the mountains of California stooped over plates of meat you helped to slaughter, on your eighteenth hour of breakneck labor, wiping beads of sweat from your brow while plating for a room full of diners who have traveled just to taste your food. All the charts and graphs and data gathered in books questioning the efficacy of the small, local farm movement pale next to the magenta-gold skies of an Oregon dawn on the morning of a farm visit.

LOVE of food *must* be at the root of food justice and food politics. To change the food world, one must be OF the food world. Respect and admiration for the natural gifts of the earth and centuries of human knowledge do not lead to growing things out of season, importing them from far-flung orchards leaving Bigfoot-sized carbon prints, or any plans for mass production of my creations. No, they call me to places of origin. They call me to meet faces, shake hands, and dip my toes into each widening pool of wisdom encountered. My projects have not only been guided by my ethics and ideals but have come full circle to fully characterize the way I live my life. I traded a stable home, romantic partnership, and financial security for a life in airports and bus stations, cushions on unfamiliar floors, and many thankful months of moons in the back of a Volvo wagon.

Once I started sourcing directly through small farms, the experience of connecting the dots from live animal to plate of mind-blowing meat was the only way to answer my own questions about the ethical and moral implications of meat eating. The people I work with are survivors for simply existing in the face of big business and prohibitive regulations, and they're saviors by virtue of the fact that they sacrifice large profit margins, physical labor, and years upon years of their time to feed YOU.

I've cooked in more than thirty-five different kitchens and in one year alone traversed the North American continent from east to west twenty-seven times. Food calls me from every corner of the world. It doesn't just say, "Come, taste me." It says, "Come, know me. Listen to me. Learn from me. Change me. Shape me. Let me make you."

Exposure to people like the Parkers, Magruders, and Decks (introduced below) has undeniably informed my work. I am humbled to share my reflections on just a few of those pivotal days, as well as give a window into the odd existence I've carved out over the years as a traveling chef. The rest of this chapter will take you through a few of my most precious memories and revelatory moments.

Heritage Breed Supper Club: Red Wattle Pig

September 2009

Heritage Farms Northwest: Jim and Wendy Parker
Forty-Five Acres in Dallas, Oregon

This farm visit was my very first as the Ethical Butcher. I had been hoping to start working with farms when I moved back west. It took me just a few days to contact over a dozen nearby farms, but as soon as I read the response from Wendy Parker, I knew I wanted to work with her and her husband right away. Personable, open, and inviting, the Parkers invited me down for a family event, a Labor Day pig roast.

Ally, my girlfriend at the time, who was still living in Brooklyn, flew in, and we drove down to Dallas—a small town in central Oregon about an hour and a half south of Portland. We got a little lost on the way to the farm, but getting lost in the rolling hills of the Willamette Valley isn't necessarily a bad thing. As we found our way to the gravel driveway leading to the Parkers' forty-five-acre farm, we were both awestruck and excitedly anticipating the day ahead. We parked in front of the quintessential big barn and exited the Volvo to be first greeted—or should I say confronted—by two Narragansett toms, or male turkeys. If there is one thing that I've picked up on my farm visits, it's that one should never get too close to toms without an insurance policy. On Jim and Wendy

Parker's farm, this policy comes in the form of a "turkey stick," which Wendy waved in her hands as she came down from the house to meet us. This stick never touches the turkeys—it doesn't have to. They aren't the smartest of barnyard creatures; waving it around in their general direction does the trick.

Wendy introduced herself and was soon joined by her husband, Jim. From there we went right to meeting the residents of Heritage Farms Northwest: Narragansett turkeys, Buckeye and White chickens, American Curly horses, and some cattle for personal consumption. Meeting the entire cast of players was a treat, but I was there for the stars of the farm—the Red Wattle pigs. The Red Wattle pig is extremely rare (about 870 were registered worldwide in 2009), and at the time, the Parkers were the only farmers in Oregon raising them. Each heritage breed is valued for different characteristics. In the case of the Red Wattle, it is both their calm demeanor and their deliciously lean meat. The difference in taste and texture is appreciated most in the belly of this traditional "bacon pig."

The Parkers first introduced us to Big Momma, a sow who had just given birth to the last litter of the year. We resisted the temptation to pick up her cute little piglets, as Jim assured us that is the one way to get these normally easygoing pigs to show you the business. We went on to meet the mixed herd of that year's previous litters, including Wilbur, a boar who would become several flavors of my hazelnut-finished bacon later that year. Red Beard, the hefty boar who so graciously supplied genetic mate-rial for that year's litters, came over for a nice rubdown as Jim told me that these pigs can get up to seventeen hundred pounds, almost THREE times the size of this guy. With the image of a car-sized boar in our heads, Ally and I were then left to wander the farm for a bit.

We watched a quarrel between a rooster and a turkey for a while and mused over what it could be about. Then I closed my eyes to take in the smells and sounds of the farm. I let the sounds of toms puffing air and ruf-fling feathers, pigs grunting, chickens clucking, and the fresh breeze fully envelope me in the sensation of *living*. I breathed in deeply, smiling in the September sunset. When Wendy called out to us, "It's time," we both knew what "time" it was. We'd come for a ground-roasted Red Wattle, and a ground-roasted Red Wattle was ready to be eaten. After hearing about the rarity of this breed, one may wonder why we were eating one. As some of the few farmers working to bring this pig back from extinction, the Parkers are careful to use only the best of the best for breeding, to ensure a strong gene pool. We learned that we'd be eating Einstein because he'd turned out to have a heart murmur. Due to the genetic defect, he didn't make the cut for breeding.

Jim Parker had fought and cursed the torrential rains of that autumnal Oregon Saturday morning to excavate a large four-by-eight-foot pit for roasting Mr. Einstein. By evening, about eight hours had passed and over one hundred pounds of pig lay under eighteen inches of dirt, cornhusks, grape leaves, burlap, aluminum foil, and rocks. Under the stares of about fifty hungry eyes, people took turns digging, and the smells of wood smoke and dirt filled the air. It was a tantalizing aroma of earth-cooked food, something most of us had never smelled before. After several rounds of digging, the burlap and chicken wire supporting the pig were visible, and four guys knelt down to grab the pig by the cage of wire cradling it. The hog was lifted up onto the ground next to the pit, and with one more heave, the hog lay on the table to a round of applause. Hardly able to contain ourselves, we began the big reveal. Blowing on our steam-burned fingers, we impatiently peeled back the layers of foil to take in Einstein in all his glory.

After a few test cuts, Jim Parker bestowed me with the greatest honor: carving Einstein. I had yet to cut a whole pig, but I was more than willing, if a little nervous, to take the helm. As soon as that knife was in my hand, I was in my element. I joined him in cutting. Gorgeous, juicy slabs of pork seemed to melt off the carcass. I found myself answering questions about various cuts, describing where the chops were going to be, and pointing out the tenderloin. I stopped to admire the marbling of the belly, which is of special interest to me for bacon curing, and pointed out the heavenly striations of fat and meat in mouthwateringly perfect proportion to one another. In my post-vegetarianism, there are times when I see how far I have come. Eating meat directly from the body of a pig, as his friends and family root around fifty yards away, and talking to the farmers who raised him—this was one of those moments.

I sliced chops while talking with the dairy farmer from down the road who supplies the Parkers with whey for their pigs—an Australian woman who raises laying chickens and cattle for meat and dairy. She spoke of a carpool of Portlanders who take turns driving down to pick up milk from her farm. She explained that the wait list for the eggs of her seventeen chickens was long and that she could do more with more chickens, but she refused to compromise the quality and sustainability of the hand-powered farm. This comment filled with me with so much respectful admiration. I was reminded that these were the farmers I wanted to meet—farmers who realize that making an extra buck at the expense of the animals they raise is unfair and unnecessary.

The full impact of what I was doing didn't really hit me until I finally stopped to take a fork to the pig's jowl, dig into some tender flesh, and feed it to Ally. As I fed her what was possibly the best meat either of us had ever eaten, I saw nothing but joy on her face. I felt so connected to life. When I told friends of my plans for this day, many asked, "How can you meet those animals and then eat one?" My answer was, "How could I not?" Even Ally thought she would have a difficult time with this day. Just because she was often a captive audience for my diatribes about meat eating didn't mean she was gung ho for dinner on the farm. As Jim and I cut, we hatched plans for curing bacon for a big Sunday brunch and breaking down big game together in the coming months. Jim then told me of his recent deal with a hazelnut grower to have a few of his pigs, including my bacon-bound pig Wilbur, clean up acres of hazelnuts a few miles up the valley.

Similar to the Iberian hams made from pigs finished on acorns, this was sort of a Northwest version that I nearly jumped out of my skin thinking about. The marbling and flavor that the already delicious meat would take on were just too much to imagine. My mind began racing with flavors for that's fall's big bacon cure as we finished. It was nearly dark by the time Jim and I were done, and everyone was inside eating. We shook greasy hands over the heap of skin and bones left for stocks and turned toward the house. We took off our muddy shoes at the door and joined the feast inside. Sitting down to the multigenerational table, I could only hope this experience would become a normal part of this butcher's life.

When Ally and I stepped out of the house hours later, the close-to-full moon was shining down on the sleeping farm. We wondered aloud how the animals put themselves to bed as we walked to the car, no longer on watch for the toms. We drove away very slowly, taking it all in. The whole drive home, I just kept repeating, "What a good day."

The menu for that first HBSC dinner is long lost to the greasy gods of the kitchen that have ruined more than a few prized handwritten recipes. Here I give the menu for the bacon that Wilbur became for my first BCN/PDX tasting party:

THE BACON GOSPEL: BCN/PDX SIP & SWILL

Five flavors of bacon served open face on fresh, local breads, paired with a handmade condiment.

LEKKAR

Tao of Tea licorice root tea, honey, and white pepper with vanilla bean and white pepper compound butter

BACKYARD MEMORIES

gin, raspberry jam, fresh sage, and Lilla Farm lavender with sage aioli

CHEAP DATE

House Spirits Distillery whiskey, triple ginger (fresh, ground, and crystallized), serrano chiles, and lime with avocado mayo

COLONEL MUSTARD WITH THE CLOVE

Extracto Roasters' Ethiopian Sidamo coffee, cherry jam, mustard seed, and cloves with cherry mustard

FINCA VISTA HERMOSA

Guatemalan microlot Micheloy coffee, cacao, vanilla bean, guajillo chiles, and cinnamon with chili orange and cilantro compound butter

Heritage Breed Supper Club: Icelandic Lamb

February 2010

Dolce Farm and Orchards: Annie Kosanovic Brown
Fifty Acres in Newberg, Oregon

Spring lamb! My first spring back in Oregon had me scheming all sorts of events. Coming off the Red Wattle dinner back in December, I was ready to get another whole animal dinner going. My search for local, heritage breed lamb led me to Dolce Farm and Orchards. Annie Kosanovic Brown opened her Willamette Valley wind-powered farm and home to me and a friend who was visiting from New York City. We surveyed her land from the driveway as Annie pointed out the acres of Italian plum trees and hazelnuts planted back in the 1920s that surrounded the house and fields of animals. Annie then invited us into her kitchen. We were drawn in by aromas of citrus and spices and, after removing our shoes, we rounded the corner of the hall to find the stove packed with pans busy stewing lamb shanks. We sat at the table and awaited the spread Annie was preparing for us. We headed out to the fields to meet everyone, including the purpose of my visit, her Icelandic sheep.

Prized for their wool as well as their meat, this breed is over one thousand years old. It was a staple for the Vikings—the pelts, fleece, and wool of the Icelandic had much to do with their success, as the Vikings made sails, ropes, and clothing from this breed. The meat is tender and delicate. As we approached the field, guard llama number 1 sat judiciously near the gate, charged with protecting the ewes and ewe lambs. We were granted access and entered the field shared by the ewes and a flock of Delaware chickens. Dozens of eyes watched us as the ewes contentedly chewed their cuds and ewe lambs played in a pile of hay nearby. We walked on and peeked into the chicken house. A few freshly laid eggs were waiting to join us for lunch. I reached in and grabbed them, thanked the ladies, and we continued. We were once again eyed by guard llama number 1 as we left the field and headed down to meet the rams and ram lambs. The Icelandic sheep is known for its dramatically curled horns, which grow in toward the face in a large corkscrew. The ram with the biggest horns stood out right away. Mr. Salty's imposing figure was amplified by his bright coat as he watched us walk by. His field was guarded by guard llama number 2, Bella. We continued on to meet the ram lambs, one of which was to be the lamb for my upcoming events in Portland. He was one of only four that would be slaughtered that season. Getting meat like this always feels special because farms this small don't sell to markets or restaurants; they sell directly from the farm. Three to four lambs a season— that's maybe eight over the course of the entire year! Talk about lowering production! This element lends such an air of novelty to meat from rare heritage breeds. The rams were skittish and turned their backs to us, so I got only a glimpse of my guy's face. I lagged behind for a moment to watch him.

Did he know who I was? Did he know why I was there?

It is these moments of clarity and accountability I am fortunate to have in my post-vegetarianism. Here I am, encompassed by this incredible farm and looking at a happy lamb frolicking with his lamby friends, knowing that in just a few weeks, he will be skinless and slack jawed, stripped of his just-budding horns, on my table awaiting my first cut. It really was an Elton John moment. The circle of life is so tangible at times. Whenever we stand between life and death, whether it be at a deathbed, to witness a birth, or just before taking a life deliberately—we are at an undeniable precipice, another kairos moment. When we kill for food, it is not honorable. It is natural. The fantastic difference between our species and all others is our ability to choose what we eat. We are not subject to pure limbic drive. We think. We internalize, rationalize, and analyze. I wouldn't pretend to know what a tiger is thinking before it begins a hunt, or what a python is thinking as is suffocates its prey, but I doubt they are having existential debates before engaging in the acts that sustain them. For me, for my human brain, there was reasoning and guilt and *feelings* far before the slaughter was to take place. I was standing yards away, eye to eye with this young ram, in full ownership of the fact that I had just requested his death. It was a surreal energetic exchange that I wish every omnivore could have. I said a quiet "Thank you" in his direction before turning away to follow after Annie.

After meeting everyone on the farm, Annie suggested we head back inside for lunch. We had no idea of the splendor that lay ahead. Over hours of conversation, we leisurely enjoyed mutton summer sausage, mutton fresh sausage with white wine and garlic, an omelet with fresh herbs from the garden, tomato-orange braised lamb shanks, and butter biscuits with Annie's home-made Italian plum jam and chutney with a mind-blowing carrot flower honey she got from a local beekeeper. Made from bees that pollinated carrot flowers and as dark as molasses, it was the richest honey I'd ever tasted. I still compare every honey to that first bite of buttery, savory, honey-drenched biscuit. Annie's generosity was matched only by the quality of the food she shared with us. After lunch, Annie showed us the pelts, raw fleece, and hand-spun yarn that she makes and sells from her farm. Bellies still full of the lambs that wore these skins, we touched the pelts slowly. The "head-to-tail" idea doesn't stop at the plate.

HERITAGE BREED SUPPER CLUB:
ICELANDIC LAMB

SAVORY LAMB BAKLAVA AND STUFFED DATES

Pita, labneh, and tabouli Tea, five-spice,
and Italian plum-roasted rack of lamb

COCOA-RUBBED SPARERIBS

with Aleppo pepper and orange glaze

DUKKAH LOIN CHOP

with roasted fennel and mint coulis Tagine
with candied pumpkin and herb-pistachio rice

SCOTCH ICE CREAM

The Bacon Gospel: Bacon for the Sound
April 2010
Deck Family Farm: Christine and John Deck
Three Hundred and Twenty Acres in Junction City, Oregon

The day at Deck Family Farm started with a surprise. John Deck's tall, thin frame waved us down in the distance as we pulled into the long driveway after a two-hour drive from Portland. I had been making bacon for the Decks for a few months and was looking forward to introducing John and Christine, his wife and the backbone of the farm, to Ally and Marissa Guggiana, an author who was following me around for a few days for a book she was writing about butchers. I was expecting to pick up a round of bellies for curing and to teach a chicken butchery lesson requested by a close friend of the Deck family. A fifteen-year-old girl who said she was interested in becoming a butcher had asked Christine to arrange it, so we planned a big chicken dinner to make use of the lesson. However, when we were introduced, much teenage giggling turned into a total denial of any such request. It was no matter, because the day had much more in store for us. Apparently, my trip was going to include a lesson in chicken slaughter for me. John motioned for Marissa, Ally, and me to follow him, I assumed to where the carcasses were waiting. There they were most certainly waiting, *cluck-clucking* away in a small cage on the ground. This would be the day I had been waiting for: my first slaughter.

I was a little shocked and more than apprehensive. I hadn't quite mentally prepared myself for this day. It had not even been two years since I had started eating meat and practicing butchery, but I had been looking forward to this occasion the entire time. I knew that taking a life would be the definitive test of my post-vegetarianism. Would I recoil and repent? Would I feel ashamed or become heartless? This test was an elusive step in getting closer to taking full responsibility for my meat consumption and the praxis of my budding food philosophy.

Up to that point I had seen the animals only when they were alive and then a week later when I picked them up from the small slaughterhouse most of my Portland-area farms used. I had yet to take the life of anything larger than a cricket with my own hands and had been writing and discussing the ethics of eating meat for a year. Could I kill for food?

I was nervous, but nerves only serve to fortify me. I loathe fear and self-doubt. If I find myself afraid to move forward, I don't turn around; I take a deep breath and march ahead. Sometimes this personality trait is a fault, but more often it has been my saving grace. I was rapt with attention even as my heart pounded in my throat. I watched the roosters peck at the grass under their cage as John talked. I can't say his words rose above the fact that I was going to turn them into food in a matter of minutes, but suddenly his voice broke through the internal dialogue.

"Ready?" John asked.

"Yep," I replied as I reached into the cage to carefully and swiftly grab a rooster around his wings. As one would expect, he was powerful, but handling birds in this firm way keeps them composed, relaxed, and safe. Allowing him to flutter and flap would end in a stressed-out and possibly injured rooster and a nice smattering of claw marks for me. Quickly carrying the rooster over to the killing cones lining one crossbeam of the killing shed, I turned him upside down and placed him head-first into the cone. Essentially a traffic cone turned upside down with an enlarged hole at the tip, the killing cone does a few things to speed up the process and make it more humane. The shape of the cone cradles the birds in a way that settles them. Just like when you do a headstand, gravity draws much of the blood to their heads and makes them a bit woozy. This position also greatly reduces the time it takes for them to bleed out once their veins are slit. The method is thus more humane not only in its treatment of their bodies but also in the clean swiftness of their passing. I put two more roosters in the cones as John did the same and stood back to take in the full landscape of six serenely dazed roosters unknowingly awaiting death.

John took a small knife out of his pocket and grabbed one rooster around the head, holding the rooster's neck between his thumb and fingers, with the neck bent against his thumb to expose the veins we would be targeting. One last humane consideration: darkness. Two quick cuts to the artery on each side of the neck, and blood was pouring into the bucket below. The rooster was gone in seconds. John did another in the same manner. His two examples rocked with postmortem nerve firing as the dogs licked the blood that splashed onto the ground. John's bloody hand passed me the knife, and I went for the third rooster. I steadied my nervous knife hand as I enclosed the rooster's head in the final quiet of my fist. I held its neck firmly and turned it slightly to expose the vein. One quick pass of the small sharp blade and an immediate pass of the knife on the other side, and it was over. Without stopping, I repeated the process three more times, ending up with a row of six headless roosters waiting to be plucked and eviscerated. People always ask how I felt in that moment.

Wasn't I afraid? Didn't I feel bad for killing an animal?

In that moment, it was not my place to be fearful or anxious. Egotistically letting my fear become hesitation only hurts the animal that deserves my full attention and respect. It would be unfair to pretend that the moment is hard for me. The moment of slaughter is about the animal, not about the human who will be walking away from that knife and its sharp edge to continue living, partially through taking life.

What is there for *me* to fear?

Humane slaughter is an idea that gets many people up in arms. Humane slaughter does not mean animals enjoy dying or that roosters feel great about being upside down for the last seconds of their lives. What it means to me is that in addition to giving animals the best life possible before slaughter, you take every step to ensure that the last few minutes are as free of stress and fear as possible and that the slaughter itself is fast and fleeting. When one thinks of the "chicken with its head chopped off" or other common chicken slaughter images—swinging them around by their necks, wringing their necks with your BARE HANDS, stepping on broomsticks placed over their necks, sticking them in small gas chambers: all traditional and contemporary means of slaughter—it is clear why the killing cone is agreed to be the most humane method among poultry processors who seek a quick, clean, and respectful death.

The Decks had invited a few family friends to join us, and four of their five children were gathered around the table for a late lunch of farm-fresh chicken. Due to rigor mortis, the roosters we had just killed would be tough for the next few days. Though completely safe to eat immediately, most animals are allowed to chill for anywhere from a day to several weeks after slaughter before being cut for retail or restaurant use. We all knew that our plan for grilling up a bunch of chickens that Christine had taken out of the deep freezer the day before would not involve these heartier roosters. But we all wanted to taste the fruits of that day's labor, so we had thrown one into the mix with the already marinating chickens from a previous slaughter. Just as expected, the fresh rooster meat stood out among the plates of tender, juicy charred flesh of the birds that had had time to relax postmortem. The newly killed rooster was dark, stringy, and chewy. We all laughed about our little experiment and finished our plates. The dogs running around the table full of kids and friends made me feel like we had known each other for years. The generosity of the Deck family was more than appreciated and made for a memorable day with Marissa. She wanted to see what I was up to with all this "Ethical Butcher" talk, and I got to show her exactly what a perfect day in my life looked like. However, our immersion into the cycle of life that day would be impossibly thorough and was nowhere near complete.

Christine led the other guests and I on an after-meal walk to the far end of the 320-acre farm as the family went about the evening chores of putting the farm to bed. We were following the goats back up the gravel road that traverses the property on its way to the house and barns, watching John shift the cloud of beef cattle from one paddock to another in the distance as we rounded the bend near their home. We were all startled as the two youngest Deck daughters came running down the dirt and gravel road, kicking up trails of dust. They shouted that two calves had just been born. Christine thought they had to be mistaken: the two pregnant heifers she had weren't expected to give birth for another one and two weeks, respectively.

We eagerly set out for the opposite side of the property, a trail of farmers and farm visitors alike, in search of signs of new life. We had to take the shortcut through the pigs and stopped to give a few back scratches along the way. Durocs and Hamps snorted and rooted, attending to their piggy affairs. One followed us noisily as we left the barn and began crossing the field behind the pig barn, our escort. With moms and babies finally in sight about a hundred yards away, the caravan forged on until a muddy bog attempted to foil our plans. We pressed ahead undaunted as our swiney escort lost interest and turned back.

For us humans, the poetic experience of witnessing death and life in such proximity was magnetic. Our soggy socks would not keep us from the golden calves that lay ahead. The group was ecstatic yet calm as we approached. We could see the two calves measuring the strength of their legs as their mothers munched grass. They weren't the least bit wary of us, a good feeling when you are near two tons of mommy cow. With the sun almost behind the ridge of the Coast Range, Christine said we had to get the new calves into the warmth of the barn right away so they could sleep inside and be checked out by a vet in the morning.

Now we were going to see what life on a farm entailed. It took three times as long to cross the muddy bog with two birth-weary heifers and two unskilled calves. We split into teams and focused on herding the mothers in hopes that the calves would follow. Know what won't move if it doesn't want to? A nine-hundred-pound cow that just gave birth. Migrating at a molasses pace, we made it to the last hill of the paddock just as the sun was slipping behind the big barn. I followed Christine's lead as she picked up and carried one of the seventy-pound calves up the steep hill before the gravel road that led to the barn. Like a 4-H dreamboat of a matriarch, with the sun's final golden rays lighting her glistening face and the flyaways of her curly loose ponytail just as it made the soft fur of the calves glow, Christine hadn't just shown me a day on her farm. She had led me on a pilgrimage.

The Deck's pork went into what is still one of my favorite events of the entire Ethical Butcher project, a bacon tasting held after hours in my aunt's cookie factory:

THE BACON GOSPEL:
BACON FOR THE SOUND SWEET MEATS

Five flavors of bacon inspired by cookie recipes, served open face on fresh bread and paired with a condiment.

PASTELITOS DE BODA

inspired by Mexican wedding cookies

Ground almonds, vanilla bean, cinnamon,
and powdered sugar with blackberry mustard

FLEUR DES BOIS

inspired by lavender sugar cookies

Lilla Farms lavender, jasmine flowers, New Amsterdam gin, and juniper berries with vanilla-chamomile compound butter

OLD OVERHOLT & OATS

inspired by oatmeal cherry cookies

Clear Creek Distilleries kirschwasser, Old Overholt rye whiskey–soaked Bing cherries, bergamot zest, white pepper, star anise, and rolled oats with citrus-mint compound butter

FIRST SNOW

inspired by ginger snaps

House Spirits Distillery whiskey, triple ginger (ground, fresh, and
crystallized), orange zest, black pepper, nutmeg, brown sugar, and
molasses with serrano chili and cacao aioli

MOLE!

inspired by double chocolate walnut cookies

Ground Belgian cacao, 77 percent dark chocolate, habanero and
serrano peppers, jalapenos, ground walnuts, ground sesame seeds,
grounds pepitas, molasses, allspice, cinnamon, anise seed, and garlic
with avocado mayonnaise

Heritage Breed Supper Club:
Local Heritage Feast

June 2010

Magruder Ranch: Mac Magruder and Ben and Grace Provan
Twenty-Four Hundred Acres in Potter Valley, California

A chilly summer sunrise met Ally and me as we packed the car for our journey, full of anticipation for the idyllic drive we'd be taking down the Oregon and Northern California coasts. We would be camping our way through miles of Pacific coastline for a week before pulling into sustainable meat veteran Mac Magruder's legendary twenty-four-hundred-acre ranch in Potter Valley, California, for my first big on-farm dinner. We emerged from the cool cover of the Valley of the Giants to find the heat of the Mendocino Valley a welcoming excitation. The surprised look on the faces that opened the door to find me—a short, heavily tattooed, baby-faced guy with a side-cocked hat and Ray-Bans—was a reaction I have grown used to over the years. Often looking more ready for the beach than a weekend of slaughter and cooking, I relish the perpetual proving of myself that has become the norm as I travel around the country doing these events and meeting people I consider to be heroes.

My connection to Mac began the very first time I sent plates around a Portland ballroom full of fifty people wondering who this Ethical Butcher guy was. After a meal that featured various cuts of Wilbur, the pig I met on my very first sourcing trip to a farm just months before, a young couple came up to me and introduced themselves and their gorgeous baby girl. Keith and Kate Feigin had come up from Northern California to attend the dinner and were beekeepers in Mendocino Valley. The couple invited me to come down for an event on their farm the following summer. These offers have now become fairly common after lectures and dinners, but this was the first. Keith and Kate had included another young couple, Ben and Grace Provan of Magruder Meats, in our plan. They had offered their ranch house as a location for the dinner and would be providing the meat. Everything fell together as the five of us organized the details of the dinner over conference calls. By the time June rolled around, I had put together a couple of events in the San Francisco Bay Area and Mendocino Valley and was planning a month-long road trip.

For over thirty years, Mac Magruder has been pasture raising his cattle, surrounded by the cliffs and rolling hills of California's Mendocino Valley. Mac is lean, tall, and rugged—impressive in a way one would expect a seasoned California cattle rancher to be. He wears Wrangler's and keeps the unruly shocks of his white hair tucked neatly under his cowboy hat.

His eyes conveyed a vast depth of knowledge even as they skeptically assessed mine. It was the familiar sizing up I've found to be common among tradespeople of all kinds. Tattoo artists, carpenters, chefs—we all doubt the next guy knows anything. I was used to this, but Mac's assessment seemed a little more incredulous than most. I knew I'd have to win him over if I was going to learn anything from him over the next few days. His oldest daughter, Grace Provan, and her husband, Ben, had both recently returned to the farm after completing degrees at Cornell University. They had just been married on the ranch two weeks before and were now working full-time on bringing a new vision to the ranch. It was Grace and Ben who had invited me for this first in a series of dinners they'd be hosting on the ranch.

Neighbors and family laughed at Mac decades earlier when he took over the ranch, which had been home to a horse camp and orchards of fruit trees, and told everyone he wanted to do pastured beef. He tells of a time when he couldn't *give* his lean, flavorful, grass-fed beef away. Years later, his grass-fed beef is the gold standard in California, and the fifth generation of Magruders is helping to take the ranch into its next stage of life. While Mac continues to spend his days out in the fields with his working dogs and animals, Grace and Ben work with eco-tourism groups, local chefs, and others to reach out to more customers.

This is an introduction to a new narrative of the American family farm. Here, two Ivy league–educated and enthusiastic young people have chosen to begin their lives together by continuing to work the land that has been supporting their family for more than a century. Returning to the life that so many in preceding generations had bucked against when they threw in the rural

towel and went Team Urban, the Magruders didn't rein-
vent the wheel. They chose to use traditional methods to
take their family's resources into the next century—doing
their part to ensure there's a sixth, seventh, and eighth
generation of Magruders on this ranch. This is real life
where change lives, not in the profitable "green" industry but in the hearts and homes of those who are simply
reclaiming traditions.

Ben, who is as deceptively cherubic as I am, and I hit
it off right away. We were excited to hammer out the
last few details over beers in the sun. Nervous anticipation changed to the antsy exuberance that often takes
over when the real preparation begins. Here's where the
addiction kicks in, the fix I am always looking for. When
people add the phrase "farm to table" to an event, they
are rarely referring to an actual experience of immersion
in farm life. Yet that is precisely how most of my events
start—covered in the blood of an animal that will become
five courses on my next menu. There is nothing like being
surrounded by the smells of a working farm. Taking an
active part in both the cycle of life and the food chain
feeds my spirit on a limbic level, an evolutionary leftover
from our humble hunter-gatherer beginnings.

In the weeks leading up to the dinner, we had hours-
long calls that revolved solely around how to break up
two animals among the six courses and thirty-five gift bags
that we'd fill with pastured meat for each diner to take
home. After we discussed the heavy agenda of the next
two days, Ben led me into the house. We walked through

a hallway filled with Mac's wooden sculptures and into the spacious kitchen. A *vittelone*—a young grass-fed beef akin to veal—lay in wait before I could even put down my bags. Preparation for the six-course ranch dinner that I would be presenting the next day would have to begin right away. I was ready for that, but rounding the corner to find a young steer on the epic butcher block that ran the length of the galley-style kitchen after driving for hours was still a surprise. I had never done a dinner of this caliber and was acutely aware of my feigned confidence. But in my usual fashion, I shrugged it off. While I had been hired off a recommendation from Keith Feigin, none of them had ever attended the handful of events I had done in Portland by that point. That young cow was the first opportunity to show the skill that belies my youthful face.

In the traditional Italian method, vittelone calves are allowed to nurse and wean on a natural timetable and begin foraging for themselves weeks before slaughter. This process not only gives the animal time to grow naturally and uninterrupted—a far cry from confinement-raised, milk-fed veal—but gives the meat a unique deep pink color and a tender, light beefy flavor. Concentrating on whole animal events means that beef is very rarely on my menus. It had been nearly a year since I had touched a cut of beef, and I had never cut a whole steer before. I was determined, though, not to let my inexperience make me doubt the knowledge I *did* possess. I looked over the carcass, making mental notes of the differences in the anatomy from a full-grown steer and starting to create the mental map that guides my knife hand in its excision and excavation.

As the mental map crystallized, I stepped away to wash my hands and take a few minutes to do a bit of mirror coaching. I actually find this tool invaluable before events and performances. Splashing water over my flushed face, I took several deep breaths, muttering "you know this" to myself. Beads of sweat returned almost immediately in the midday heat, and I watched them form and run down the sides of my face, almost meditating on the path of the stream as the drops joined together. More cool water and one last affirmation, and I walked into the kitchen, briskly removed the muslin that covered the carcass, and started cutting. The age and size of the steer made cutting it a new challenge. The anatomy dictated that I used a blend of veal, pork, and beef techniques to get the best cuts off the carcass. It was actually becoming a bit of a game. What do I do with the shoulder? Treat it like lamb and pork and keep the subprimal big, or treat it like a beef chuck and piece out every steak? I finally felt at ease when I made it to the hindquarters, the round. I had cut my butcher's teeth on legs of beef. Heaving the 120-pound limbs over my shoulder and breaking them down for all the ground beef and sirloin for the shop was my job every day for my first meat-cutting year, so those final cuts were a cinch.

As I made my way through the carcass, I got word that everyone was gathering across the creek for the slaughter of the two pigs I'd be butchering. Even while I was working on an entire carcass, I could not resist witnessing my first pig slaughter. I covered the vittelone with a few towels and ice packs, grabbed some beer for everyone, and headed down to the outdoor slaughter site Mac had rigged. USDA regulations prohibit farmers from selling meat they've slaughtered on their own farm. However, since we'd be eating the meat on the farm, this was an opportunity for everyone to learn from Mac, who'd been slaughtering for personal use longer than most of us had been alive. We gathered around the fire with family and friends, working dogs and pigs. The air around us was charged with electricity as we waited for Mac to give the word that we were ready to start. I passed the beers around and went to check out the two pigs calmly munching at hay in a nearby trailer, rightfully oblivious and unaware of their impending fate.

Since we were doing this dinner on the ranch, we were not under regulation of the USDA. In most cases, meat that is sold and served to the public must be killed and processed in a USDA facility. However, on the farm, the farmer makes the rules. Farmers can choose to raise, kill, and eat the animals raised in any manner they see fit, as long as consumption occurs on the farm and does not constitute animal cruelty. In processing plants, where dozens to thousands of animals are processed daily, pneumatic and electric guns are used for killing, but for farmers and hunters out on the land, firearms and knives are the preferred tools. For a big animal like a pig, shooting is absolutely the quickest and least stressful way to go. Using a knife, as we had with the roosters, would require a chase and a wrestling match with the pig that would frighten and possibly injure both farmer and pig. That is a death match, not humane slaughter. Mac is an excellent marksman and controlled the scene with ease. These pigs were seconds from their death and the air was calm. I watched Mac raise his gun, point it squarely between the eyes of the first pig, and POP! The pig fell like a cardboard cutout. Mac immediately pulled it out of the trailer and onto the ground, then slit its jugular vein. Pigs are roughly the size of large people at slaughter weight, and I realized right in that moment that everything I knew about what dying looks like came from TV and movies. The pig *had* fallen as if transformed into stone, eyes glazed. However, the nerves of its body fired at will for another two minutes. It was like the overacted final death scene of an old western. It had all happened so swiftly that the other pig was still chewing on his treats when the next POP! came. The process was repeated with the second pig, and within a cool ten minutes, two pigs lay dead, a small pool of blood under the neck of each.

Ally took photos as I stared at the carcasses. I was transfixed, going over the events in my head over and over again. The small details were the most interesting: the almost comedic manner in which each pig had fallen, the remarkable color of blood-stained grass, and the smell of a freshly discharged firearm. The image of feathered sanguine spouts flooded my mind as I stared into the glass eyes of the bleeding swine. The blood on the grass was much like the blood splatters on the concrete that had caught my eye when I had participated in my first chicken slaughter just two months before on the Deck Family Farm in Oregon. I had dealt with many of my apprehensions about taking life on that day, and now I was building on those victories over fear by taking part in the killing of something much bigger, stronger, and smarter than any chicken.

"We should all have it so good," Mac said.

In the time I had gotten lost in reliving that memory, the pigs had finished bleeding out. His words ripped me out of my wistfulness and rung with solemn truth. We *should* all have it so good. These animals lived a life many humans could never imagine: free from mistreatment, hunger, and disease, loved and cared for on thousands of acres of unfettered nature until the moment swift and certain death befell them. Very few people in this world enjoy a similar progression from cradle to grave. The argument is not about whether or not it is right to kill and eat animals. We don't eat meat because animals are unintelligent or can't feel pain. In fact, we raise, kill, and eat meat responsibly because we know these animals are sentient beings. Working with the people who fed and cared for these animals, and watching those people reclaim their investment by killing the very beings they brought into this world, is profound. They don't take pleasure in it, but they take every effort to make the death dealing short and to the point. I know farmers who give their pigs joyrides to get them used to the trailer that will ultimately take them to the slaughterhouse. Mac spends more time with his pigs and cattle than he does with any human. I thought with admiration of the hundreds, if not thousands, of times Mac had been through this process.

Mac employed his skills of improvisation to create our rustic outdoor slaughter area. A barrel of water sat boiling over a fire, with a hose nearby for adding cool water to attain the optimum scalding temperature of 140 degrees F. Plunging a carcass into scalding water aids in the removal of hair and skin from the pig and must occur at this precise temperature. Too hot, and the skin and layers of fat begin to cook; too cool, and nothing happens but an awkward bath for a dead pig. In slaughterhouses, giant machines perform this dirty task. The whole pig is placed inside a coffin-shaped washing machine–like contraption and rubber pads remove the skin as the pig is turned repeatedly in the scalding water for a few minutes.

Without these modern marvels to aid us, we'd be hoisting the nearly two-hundred-pound pigs into the barrel using a small excavator Mac had rigged with a loop of chain. I made a cut in the space between the Achilles tendon and bone of each hind leg, stuck the hooks for hanging the carcass into each hole, and affixed the hooks to the chain. We hauled the first pig up onto our makeshift rack and plunged it deeply into the barrel. Mac raised the excavator to lift the pig out of the water, and we surrounded the steaming carcass with palm-sized, metal flat scrapers to begin removing mud, skin, and hair. It was an incredibly dirty job. Debris flew in every direction as we worked furiously to scrape the skin clean. The heat of the scalding barrel of water next to us, the fire heating it, and the muddy hair shower we were getting from the carcass made this by far the hardest part of the job. Every few minutes, the skin would cool and the hair follicles would tighten their grip once again. We'd have to stop the scraping to submerge the pig to wash off the mud and dirt and reopen the hair follicles. Once the pig was mostly hairless, we all stood back as Mac took out a large knife to eviscerate the pig. Grabbing the hindquarters to steady the pig pendulum, he made one long cut from bung to rib cage. Bowels spilled out onto the ground, full of the very hay we had been watching the pig eat just minutes before. The dogs could barely stand this provocation and were finally allowed to jump on the scraps that had been taunting them.

Mac continued to cut the more securely anchored organs from the cavity, and I gathered them in a metal bowl. The liver, kidneys, and heart would all find their way into my menu the next day. I headed back to the house, hands caked in blood, mud, and pig hair, face beaming with the accomplishment of yet another post-vegetarian milestone. There was no time for reflection, only more meat to break down. I washed up, changed shirts, threw my apron back on, and finished cutting the vittelone.

After I'd wrapped the last few cuts and cleaned up the scraps of meat the dogs had missed on the floor, Ben,

Mac, Keith, and the others who had helped with the dirty work came in. We were all exhausted, famished, and absolutely filthy. We stood in a collective stupor, reeling over the amount of work we had done that day and anticipating the mountain of work that the next day would bring. Everyone headed off to one of the three bathrooms in the house to take much-needed showers, and then we piled into our cars and drove into Ukiah for a good chat at the restaurant where Mac's younger daughter, Alice, works when she's home from college.

We ordered burgers made with meat from Magruder beef, and Grace and Ben started telling me a story that would become one of my prime examples of the problems with the "green" and "sustainable" foods industry. I see their personal story as proof of the misguided and misleading green-washing of industrial food corporations, a topic of great interest to me. These unregulated terms mean something much more broad and dynamic than the government-owned "organic" label, and the transparency of the practices those terms represent is central to my work.

Months before, the Magruders and a few other local beef ranchers had been contacted by a very prominent national natural foods chain, which said it was dedicated to stocking its stores with local, grass-fed beef. As one would expect, the collective response was positive, and the group of farmers attended a meeting with the suits representing the firm. The farmers were given a list of how their animals had to be raised if this chain of green giants was to carry their products. According to Grace, the group of farmers agreed with and had in fact been exceeding most of the standards independently for years. However, one rule stopped the ranchers dead in their tracks: no castration.

The farmers looked to each other and back to the representatives of this store. Were they kidding? Did these people have any idea what they were talking about?

The corporation seemed more concerned with their customers' *perception* of the neutering process as inhumane than with the actual living conditions of the animals. The irony of people who will never step foot on a ranch being obsessed with protecting the testicles of the bulls they will eat is laughable, considering we spay and neuter dogs and cats without hesitation. Ranches and farms certainly keep a few intact bulls for breeding, but most of the male calves will go to beef. While the usual slaughter weight for beef cattle is about eleven hundred pounds, a full-grown bull will reach two to three thousand pounds. Ranchers like Mac have a few hundred head of cattle grazing their land, and it takes a year or more to bring them to slaughter weight.

Consider the reality of one, two, ten, or more intact bulls in one place. To have them all running around with Rocky Mountain oysters propelling their tonnage for a year or two is a risk to the farmers and the animals themselves. Castration reduces fighting between males and the subsequent goring or spearing with their horns of anyone in range. A few thousand pounds of angry bull can plow through just about any fence or gate, putting drivers and pedestrians at risk. Aside from this more acute risk, experienced herd management would succumb to natural laws of evolution as farmers would lose control over the husbandry, or mating, of their live-stock—putting healthy genetic lines and biodiversity at risk. This rule was insulting to a group of farmers who had been raising their cattle humanely for years, on their own terms, far before any "green" market decided it was trendy to follow the laws of nature. The ranchers told the company they'd consider its standards and reply in a few weeks. Weeks later, though, the farmers were notified that the natural foods giant had decided to import grass-fed beef from New Zealand instead—New Zealand, of course, being just a few miles up the road from the San Francisco Bay.

The company in this story implies that it is concerned with the whole food system, which naturally includes farmers. Its decision to import beef from sixty-five hundred miles away proved to me that it wasn't genu-inely interested in working with local farmers. It simply wanted the stamp of approval and the higher price point that came along with it. The line of demarcation between the methods of farms such as Mac's and hypocritical cor-porations that use labels they know customers will "like" underlines their lack of dedication to and disregard for the actual needs of farmers and their animals.

Back at the ranch house, everyone else retired and left Ben and me sitting on either side of the butcher block, drinking whiskey late into the night. It had been the kind of long day that seems like it could have been three. I'd woken up that morning far away on the misty Northern coast of California at a friend's farmhouse in Arcata and driven hours through towering western redwoods to cut an entire young steer and help slaughter two pigs for the first time. My body ached with expectation for the next day as we spoke in whispers to keep the slumbering house quiet. We arrived at what I have found to be commonplace for drunken conversations with others in the sustainability movement: abject dissolution and depressing predictions. I have literally been brought to tears over too many whiskey sodas about depleted fish populations. I realize not too many people sit around mourning overfishing or lamenting the inevitable irrelevance of any changes other than a near complete and total shift away from fossil fuels, but that's what happens. We talked until we were both nodding off between saucy ramblings, then shared the biggest bro hug I'd had in a while. I headed upstairs to collapse into bed with Ally. Staring at the ceiling as I reran the day, I listened intently to the Russian River as it bumbled along just a hundred yards from our open window, lulling me into well-deserved deep sleep in a house that has cradled this family for generations.

I was up by seven the next morning. My puffy eyes read over the menu I had written weeks before as the coffee kicked in. I had given Ben loose parameters for sourcing to have only the freshest local ingredients, so it was now time to adjust the menu to make use of everything that arrived that morning. Greens of many varieties, fennel bulbs, onions, berries, potatoes, and vittelone chops filled the refrigerator to capacity, and I hadn't even started cutting the two pigs yet. I sat down with my menu and wrote what we chefs call a prep list, a list of every task that needs to be done, roughly in order, so that all elements of all courses are done when they need to be. Cooking is an unmatched trial in time management, and it all starts with the prep list.

My way of presenting a six-course seasonal meal on a ranch means that everything, almost every step, has to be done the day of the dinner. In addition to the fridge-shaped cornucopia of produce, there were several coffin-sized coolers full of meat from the previous day's cutting. I would have to cut down only one pig because Grace's cousin Mike, who had helped with the slaughters, would be taking one whole pig to his house in Napa for a pit roast. With so much to do, I welcomed any lightening of my load. Ben watched and asked questions as I made quick work of the pig breakdown and rationing. It was like taking apart a Lego structure and passing the pieces around. I needed the hams, belly, and offal for my menu. The loin and shoulder would become chops and steaks for diners to take home. I finished the hog within the hour, wrapped up the cuts, and placed them into yet another cooler, leaving the belly out to prepare it for my smoked pork belly dish.

I pulled a basket of fresh strawberries out of the fridge, diced enough to fill a small bowl, and set it aside. I then trimmed the belly of small bones and squared off the edges so that it would both cure and smoke evenly. I covered the belly in kosher salt and strawberries, drizzled a bit of whiskey over it, and rubbed the mixture all over the belly, massaging it deep into the striated layers of fat and meat. I placed the belly in the smoker, where the heat of the smoke would turn the proteins and sugars of the meat and berries into a thick slab of melting fat and tender meat with a sweet, caramelized crust. This Maillard reaction, the result of the application of heat to any combination of amino acids and carbohydrates, is responsible for the "roasty" flavor of chocolate, coffee, and nuts. Gaining mastery of its secrets is one of my culinary holy grails. I am continuously hunting down the key to creating *meat candy*.

I sent Mike on a hunt around the property for fresh pine needle tips. Only the green new growth works for cooking, so I gave him specific instructions on the kind of needles to look for: bright green new growths, with their unsurpassed vegetal astringency, at the end of tufts of needles, which are easily pulled away from their more hardy predecessors. People often react with astonishment when they find out I've put pine needles in their food. I find the tannic quality of the thin leaves an unmatched addition to the flavor profile of this floral ham. I then gathered the lavender I had brought from Oregon, crushed some juniper berries, and found smoky Scotch that would meld the soprano notes of the floral ingredients with the guttural nuttiness of the pastured pork. The hams got a bath of these ingredients and honey from Keith's bees, while quartered fennel bulbs simmered in cream on the cherry red vintage range. I moved on to the many steps of my rose and pork liver baklava and *dukkah,* which would start the meal. The fragrant plumes from the hot, dry pan that was toasting whole cumin, coriander, and fennel seeds tickled my nose as they rose into the air.

At about six o'clock, guests began to arrive for the hour-long ranch tour Mac had included as part of the dinner. As people began to fill the house, I began my usual pacing ritual. Walking around the kitchen for a minute, reciting the menu aloud and making sure every element is done, I take this meditative moment to refocus as I transition from preparation to service. This step back from the action gives me time to either settle into high gear ready to rock or realize I've forgotten something huge and attempt a solution. Thankfully, all was in order. I donned my chef's coat like armor for battle. I leaned back against the wall to take a few deep breaths and sips of wine and map out the timing of "firing" the first courses.

Keith arrived just then with more of his honey and a jar of bee pollen that would be the garnish on the goat's milk ice cream he had made from his handful of Nubian goats. Keith insisted I try the pollen and brought over a teaspoon brimming with the golden powder. I took the whole spoonful in at once and was blown away by the buttery burst of spring in my mouth. I was so amazed, I asked for another taste. Now, small amounts of local bee pollen are supposed to be a natural antihistamine for pollen allergies. *Small amounts.*

As it turns out, this lifelong asthmatic is apparently VERY allergic to spoonfuls of spring. The pollen threw me over the histamine edge, and I would pay for those tastes of fairy dust for the entire night of service. Between introducing courses to the thirty-five glowing expectant faces gathered on the sunporch, grilling dozens of steaks at once, and plating each course, I was trying to taste vinaigrette with a plugged nose. I was forced to turn away to sneeze every three minutes and to step into the bathroom to blow my nose and wash my hands every five. It added a ridiculously comical layer of stress to the service, but food made it out and the ooh's and aah's from the packed dining room kept me going. My sinuses cleared just as the sixth course went out, and I was finally able to engage the curious crowd.

As is typical for my style of "lecture" dinner, I followed the dessert plates out, leaving the kitchen to the volunteers who were there to clean. I made my way around the room of local food writers and farmers, talking about family farms in the area. As always, there was a haze of wonder and a host of questions about my touring and my interest in heritage breed animals. Before people slowly began to trickle out of the ranch house, many stopped to watch the photo slideshow Ally had made that unapologetically portrayed the process that went into the meal they'd just enjoyed. When the last of the guests left, Ben and I shared pats on the back as we went over the comment cards that had been sent around after the meal. Thirty-five diners and the only critique?

Too much food. I find it hard to take offense to that one.

LOCAL HARVEST SUPPER CLUB
AT MAGRUDER RANCH

DUKKAH
crusted chèvre and tapenade with crostini

ROSE AND PORK LIVER BAKLAVA
made with Lovers Lane honey

STRAWBERRY PETIT SALÉ
over summer salad

WHITE WINE-BRAISED VITTELONE CHOPS
with finocchio con latte al forno and cioppolini in agrodolce

WOODLAND HERB UNCURED HAM
with wilted greens and mustard-tarragon grilled potatoes

GOAT MILK ICE CREAM
with pollen sprinkles

The Bacon Gospel:
Bacon for the Queen City

August 2010

Carriage House Farms: Richard Stewart
Three Hundred Acres in North Bend, Ohio
Mark Bodenstein and Justin Dean Relish Restaurant Group
Covington, Kentucky

In spring of 2010, I was invited to participate in a series of events with Relish Restaurant Group, some of the most driven food folks I've had the pleasure of working with. I was flown in for a few events as part of their big annual Farmer's Fair. My first "big business" trip came with all the perks: a nice hotel room, local press. A driver was even waiting for me with one of those little signs: "REED." I jumped out of his sleek black Oldsmobile and into a billowing California king overlooking the Ohio River, downtown Cincinnati twinkling back at me. I leaned back in bed with the tiny joint I'd smuggled onto my flight, lit up, and sighed a few incredulous trails of smoke. This trip felt different. I had been *hired* as some sort of "expert." It was the first time I realized that my big mouth and brazen heart were pushing me into the spotlight.

After just a few hours of rest, the meat marathon began. I woke early to meet Justin Dean, COO of the Relish Group, and Jay Denham, a farmer, butcher, and chef who would be teaching me a new butchery technique later that day, as well as hosting his own dinner as part of the fair. Before our planned day of cutting together, we would head out to Carriage House Farms to gather produce for our respective dinners.

We first took a walk around Richard Stewart's small farm, which has been in the family for generations, and then drove down to the far end of his land, past the swarming hives and requisite shooting ranges that dotted the land. Richard is like many small farmers today who are bucking conventions and going back to traditional methods of farming. As with many other agriculture-dominant states, for the past few decades, much of Ohio's land has been solely and contractually dedicated to growing corn and soy for the meat and biofuel industries. Richard is slowly converting his family's soy and cornfields back to a diverse spread of produce and grains for a community supported agriculture (CSA) program, wherein customers buy shares of a season's bounty and receive weekly baskets of produce. He also runs a local apiary with all those hives we'd passed. As he provides many of Covington's restaurants with local produce and honey, he's quickly proving neighbors and doubtful family members wrong, already projecting that 30 percent of the farm's yearly profits will come from his new venture. The doubting Toms are quieting down with every year's harvest, and he is becoming an example in the community of an alternative to raising subsidized mono crops for the commodity market.

In the bright sun of an already hot Ohio River valley morning, we jumped out of Justin's truck to help Richard harvest potatoes. Standing in a field in the Sperry Topsiders I'd found unworn at the Goodwill the week before, I weighed my options for a moment: ruin the shoes or go barefoot? Anyone who knows me knows my answer. Off came the shoes. Less than twelve hours after touching down in Kentucky, I stood with soft, freshly turned Ohio soil between my toes. Pressing deep into the still night-cool soil, I felt the sunshine awaken the nutritive magic of the earth as it warmed me. In that moment, it was all I could do to contain my excitement for what the rest of the trip would hold. I strained to stay focused. With all of us moving up and down the rows collecting the dirt-covered roots, several pounds of potato-filled milk crates quickly stacked up in the back of the truck. Potatoes picked, the three of us headed off to begin our real day: cutting two and a half pigs and a whole steer for the dinners Jay and I were each hosting on Saturday and the big festival on Sunday.

Driving back along the river, we headed to the industrial area of Covington, where Relish's commissary kitchen was located. Relish impressed me so much because it was doing something few restaurant groups have tried or can pull off successfully: sourcing everything within a one-hundred-mile radius, using whole animals, and, most impressively, working its very own pork farm to supply its six restaurants with its own carefully selected mixed breed of heritage pork. The Magruders were also working on their own breed of pork, suited specifically to the microclimate and living conditions of their ranch. Similarly, Jay and Justin were working to find just the right mix of swine to make the most of the farm they had on the West Virginia border.

That day we'd be shooting a video of Jay teaching me the Italian/Spanish method of pig butchery, a style mostly aimed toward cured meats, or charcuterie. Taking a skill that I knew very well, cutting pigs down in the American/British block style, and turning it into a brand-new learning opportunity was an eye-opening reminder of the endless learning involved with gaining skills in a trade. There are always more masters to learn from, new tricks and new techniques. With the American/British block-style cuts I was trained in, you rely on arbitrary fixed lines to delineate cuts from one another, but many other styles of cutting are dictated by the anatomy of the carcass itself. This "seam" style means less uniformity of cuts but also less waste and a wider variety of cuts, with more consistent characteristics. Surveying this carcass for new landmarks, I felt hurled back to my first day behind the counter all over again. Even if for just a little while, it was energizing and thrilling.

I'd need that energy. We would be turning the steer and two and a half pigs into pounds and pounds of sausage and burgers for the big fair on Sunday. Jay and I started in on the pork while Justin attacked the steer on the other side of the room. We would do this first half pig together so I could pick up the technique, and then we'd each break one of the remaining pigs on our own. Most of the cutting felt familiar: one to remove the head, locating the iliac crest of the pelvis and making a cut to separate the hams from the loins, and so on. It was when we got down to the individual cuts that I began learning. Jay was very focused on curing and so always cuts the shoulders and hams down in the Italian method, which yields the prized *coppa* cut and hams for prosciutto. We'd start on the hams because they were the quickest, meaning we'd be able to finish them and get them back into the cooler and out of the heat of the kitchen.

With the leg already detached from the spine at the pelvis, we'd just need to remove the pelvis to isolate the prized ham—the leg itself, starting from the femur and all that luscious fat and muscle surrounding it. Carving around the concave and convex pelvic curves, Jay had freed all but the socket of the joint. Changing the angle of attack, he made several more incisions, and the slippery red ball of the femur shone bright. He set the pelvis and its attached sirloin meat onto our pile for sausage. Grabbing the hoof and pulling the leg closer to him, Jay started doing something I'd never seen before. He began to wiggle and shake the foot, as if trying to rouse the no-longer-living pig. He then massaged the ham as he continued to shake the hoof back and forth, explaining that to cure well, he'd need to remove as much moisture as possible, including blood. This massaging and shaking action was pumping the blood out of vessels, with it all oozing out quite dramatically from the femoral artery and vein. Jay patted away the blood with a towel as it seeped out until the vessels ran dry. He started to carve the meaty side of the ham into a perfect circle with a smooth, even surface of meat and fat and skin. All of this is to ensure that the curing process occurs uniformly. I was entranced by the methodical and intentional cuts Jay made to define a cut that was as perfect geometrically as it would be gastronomically. Bryan and I could definitely be described as detail oriented, *maybe* anal, but I had never seen someone take such slow care to sculpt cuts.

Hams happily nestled in a cure of salt and spices, we moved on to the more complex shoulder. The shoulder of a pig is, in my opinion, the crown jewel of pork cuts. Yes, I'm known for bacon—pork belly is a source of mystical powers yet to be understood by humankind, we all know that—but shoulder? Pork shoulder is a knockout lady mixed-martial artist with an impeccable fashion sense who rides a motorcycle and builds five-story tree houses with her bare hands. Pork shoulder can do anything you've ever dreamed of. *Pernil*, carnitas, carne enchiladas, country ribs, pulled pork, and all manner of sausages and roasts are made from the shoulder. Bacon may get the credit for pork's popularity, but the shoulder does the work.

Jay would be teaching me a whole new way to look at the shoulder and would introduce yet another three new cuts to my repertoire: The coppa, *presse*, and *pluma*—all taken from Italian butchery. The coppa is the very beginning of the loin, the muscle that runs along both sides of the spine. It's the cut that makes melt-in-your-mouth hot coppa, sweet coppa, and other Italian cured meats.

Jay started to remove the spine and top ribs that encase the shoulder cuts and began carefully freeing a cylindrical shape out of the muscles north of the humerus and shoulder blade. Once he released this, the coppa, he cut off a very thin, narrow strip of meat called the pluma and set them both aside. The shoulder blade of the pig was now partially exposed; we'd just need to remove the blade to have a boneless shoulder for pulled pork. Jay pushed the shoulder over to me, and with a few quick passes of my knife, I freed the blade. Just as I went to throw it onto our bone pile, Jay yelled, "Wait! That's the best part!" Puzzled, I looked over the nooks and crannies of leftover flesh and cartilage hanging off the blade and wondered which of these remnants was hiding a treasure.

I tossed the blade back to Jay, and he pointed out a tiny triangle of flesh caught between two ridges of the triangular blade. With one scooping action of the flexible boning knife, a thin triangle of succulent meat was free and bound for our bellies. Jay explained that while he was studying with butchers in Italy, it was these cuts, the presse and the small pluma, that butchers kept to themselves on slaughter day. He described a scene that sounded like something from a travel guide: a sunset pig roast in the Tuscan hills with seasoned Italian butchers enjoying the tender fruits of a day's labor. As he was telling this story, Jay grilled up the two little slices of meat. To this day, those were the most lavish bites of meat I have ever enjoyed. Seared to perfection and medium-rare, juicy on the inside—a pleasure truly earned by those who have worked to find these hidden gems.

It was already late afternoon. With mouths still full of the only food we'd eaten since early morning, we turned back to work, sustained by a few ounces of the hundreds of pounds of meat we'd handle that day. We both honed our knives, transported by meditative motions again to the centered mental and physical space of cutters and creators. I remembered falling in love with butchery in the beginning in part because of the ritualistic nature of the trade. To work with death directly, feeling intimately connected to its value. To be covered in blood, the life force of other beings. Carefully choosing and caring for your tools, you learn to put metal to stone and metal. You learn to find just the right angles in relation to the stone and steel for every knife, to manipulate the blade of each unique metallic alloy into an edge so sharp that it will catch the fibrous proteins of a thumbnail. The search for the right application of pressure against the steel rod—20 degrees for one knife; 45 for another—this mastery of hand-eye coordination and muscle memory is every bit as important as learning to use the tools themselves. I sort of reveled in the nostalgia of the moment—I had spent nearly every morning of my first year of butchery sharpening all the knives that Bryan and I used. In all my solo butcher's sojourning, I had really come to miss working with other butchers, more than I had noticed. The shit talking, the air of healthy competition, pranks with animal parts—butcher culture is one unto itself. It was good to be home.

Satisfied with our tools, and with the pressa, pluma, and coppa forcing new synapses, we each reached for a whole hog and heaved them onto the cutting tables opposite one another. We both cut as quickly as we could. Justin was by this time about halfway through his steer. Standing just a bit below my five foot six, Justin was dwarfed by the containers of beef primals surrounding him. He popped up over the rib cage he was wrestling into rib eyes and asked how we were moving along with the piggies. Three flush faces wiped sweat, gave greasy meat-covered thumbs-ups, and dove back into their tasks. We'd not only need to cut these carcasses down, but we had to get all the cuts ready for both of our dinners as well as the festival. This meant cutting most of the meat into one-inch cubes. Imagine the time it takes to turn most of a twelve-hundred-pound steer into one-inch cubes. All these cubes then have to go through the grinder twice. Then burgers must be weighed and formed and sausages stuffed. Jay and I each had plans with the bellies and some of the offal, so we both had some preparation to do before the day was done as well. By the time we were cleaning the last bits of dried fat off the walls and cleaning our knives, it was just before one in the morning. The long day had turned four carcasses into food for hundreds of people and turned me and two new friends into bodies worn from over twelve hours of dismantling beasts. The only medicine for our ills was bourbon and burgers. We piled into the truck and plowed our way back to town.

The next morning, I took a walk through the tiny town of Covington before finding my way to the kitchen at Chalk Food + Wine, where I'd be running my Bacon Gospel dinner. It would be a fun day in a busy, tight kitchen. Chef Mark Bodenstein's restaurant held a separate dining room; this is where I'd be serving my private dinner to guests who had bought tickets weeks before. Chef Bodenstein prides himself on the fact that there is not one can or even *can opener* in the house. I have never seen a kitchen so improvisational. His ethos in the kitchen closely matches mine. His menus are free-form and ask diners to leave much to the chef's ability to make the most of what is available right now. It is easy to print menus when you are ordering from a supplier that will bring tomatoes every day of the year. It is much harder to predict when you base your menu on every day's best offerings. This style really means that some dishes are created spontaneously, in the middle of service. I've done it in my events, and I watched in respectful disbelief as I moved through my courses in this shared kitchen. Even during his rushed dinner service, Mark put whatever didn't get used in my plating into his free-form ingredient-driven plates being sent out. Whether it was my watermelon/pink peppercorn sauce, juniper-crusted pork loin, or purple bean hash, Mark and his kitchen found a use for it without missing a step. This innovative resourcefulness and resilient improvisation is the key to successful local sourcing and, to me, a mark of a chef's true talent.

After our respective services were completed, Mark, a new dad, went home, and I joined the after-dinner conversations in the dining room. A few friends of the restaurant had stayed to enjoy wine and conversation into the wee hours of the morning with the restaurant's GM and sommelier, and a server who was one of Covington's few bike commuters. Many meandering words through the area's history as a winemaking region to food deserts in urban centers finally led us to dragging ourselves out of Chalk and into the late-summer-night humidity. I walked back through the town square to my hotel, unsure of the dream I had begun to craft for myself.

I spent the next day continuing these discussions with the locals. Introducing myself a thousand times to the people stopping at Relish's stand at the fair and teaching a bacon curing class on a blazing hot Kentucky day, I saw in Covington a fire and a drive toward action that I had expected to come in a very different package. I was looking for a certain style of dress, academically politicized language, knowledge of micronutrients and yoga, co-op memberships—signs I would recognize from presumed great beacons of light in the sustainability movement like Portland, San Francisco, and New York. Here, in Covington, I saw people excited about change and ready to dive in to help. The people I met cared about small family farms not just because they wanted to improve local economies or fight the USDA but because these were *their* family farms. They wanted to learn to cure bacon not as a trendy foodie parlor trick but because of memories of their grandfathers curing hams and bellies in the garage. I was refreshed by the way ego was not wrapped up in their food choices as it is in some cities, where "Oh, you eat GLUTEN?!?!" could be roughly translated as: "What a helplessly bloated BARBARIAN."

We all have different interests at stake in this fight for food justice. We are all strengthened by different means of fighting, all heartened by the advances made on each front. These farmers and chefs in Kentucky are finding the path to sustainable living that works for them. As I travel around, I try to discover the right path for myself—following each new lead partially down a road before trying another. This trial and error must never be seen as a weakness. All too often in our culture, we devalue this process of finding the most effective method. We value expediency over efficiency. If we all take the time to lean back and take a wider view of where we are going, our choices become more impactful. In this wide-angle lens, you can fit yourself into what I do, what Jay Denham and Christine Deck do. This time in Covington taught me one thing: We are all working together.

THE BACON GOSPEL:
BACON FOR THE QUEEN CITY

SOUTHERN LIVING
peaches cooked in bourbon, fresh lemon, and basil

SWEETER THAN TEXAS
chocolate, cumin, cinnamon, allspice, cloves, and tomato

MORNING JULEP
strawberries macerated with bourbon and salt, mint, and
coated in cornmeal

❧ ❧ ❧

HIGHLIGHTS FROM
MY DINNER AT CHALK

DUELING SWEETER THAN TEXAS
petit salé over wilted greens (one smoked, one braised)

JUNIPER AND TARRAGON PORK LOIN ROAST
with watermelon/pink peppercorn sauce

ᴄᴏ ᴄᴏ ᴄᴏ

Though I set out in 2009 with a blog about meat consumption and ex-vegetarian pondering, I soon came to
see that I was looking at the food world only through a
meat-focused framework. This is the distracting problem
of the skewed vision that post-vegetarianism had left me
with. It was all about meat and the evils of the meat industry. However, meat eating was not the issue. Or, rather,
it was only one symptom, one element of the problem.
The more I built and expanded my projects, the more my
attention shifted toward my blind spots.

I began looking at the whole plate first, starting to move
toward fuller menus that leaned just as heavily on local
vegetables and traditional processes as the provenance of
the meats. Continuing to evolve the ideas that the Ethical
Butcher was addressing, I then looked up from the plate
altogether to focus on who is at the table. If I wanted
my work to be more accessible to my peers, I needed to
find ways to get out of the foodie-world star child role. I
began avoiding bacon events, ended my bacon club, filled
my schedule with cheap private dinners, and intensified
my transience.

Between December 2009 and December 2011, I self-
produced over ninety events, half of those private dinners,
in ten different North American cities. From June 2010,
when I began touring in earnest, to December 2011,
when I began to pull the brakes on the Ethical Butcher
train, I logged over forty-eight thousand miles in sixteen

cross-country trips and rode over twenty thousand miles of highway between San Francisco and Seattle. All of this without a credit card, trust fund, investors, or the proverbial pot of gold. These years have been the most transformative of my young life, and the changing settings of each event are surely reflected in the menus, as is a sort of documentation of the development of my personal style, as well as glimpse into the many incredible people I encountered along the way.

I am just a guy. This is just food. If I can do it, everyone can make these experiences part of their lives. Even after nearly four years of searching, I'm not ashamed to admit that I've yet to find the best balance of ethics and the realities of the industry; nor do I know everything there is to know about meat sourcing, farming, or the butchery trade. This mastery of skills will take many years to mold and shape, but knowing how to answer my own questions and how to observe and learn from my peers has helped me connect others to solutions for their own questions. Our culture is far too concerned with having answers and pays too little attention to the perpetually open nature of true learning. I have certainly become knowledgeable in a very specific way, but I actively seek out challenges to that knowledge every day. This constant questioning has been the most consistent characteristic of the Ethical Butcher projects.

(*left*) Red Wattles at Heritage Farms Northwest, including Wilbur (below) September 2009..

(*right*) In our makeshift kitchen with a view, Jim Parker and I cut freshly ground-roasted pork for our monumental meal, September 2009

A few of the Deck girls ready the grill for their homegrown chicken.

full circle on Deck Family Farms, April 2010

(*top left*) Roosters in killing cones;

(*bottom left*) Thoughtful heifers greet us after dinner;

(*above*) The newest farm resident, a newborn calf.

Another revelatory chain of events and moments with Mac suspended in time.
Magruder Ranch, June 2010

Homestyle butchery on the ranch, complete with dogs-
the Border Collie mix is my best friend of 10 years, Bronko-
sure wish he could always hang out with me in the kitchen!
Magruder Ranch, June 2010

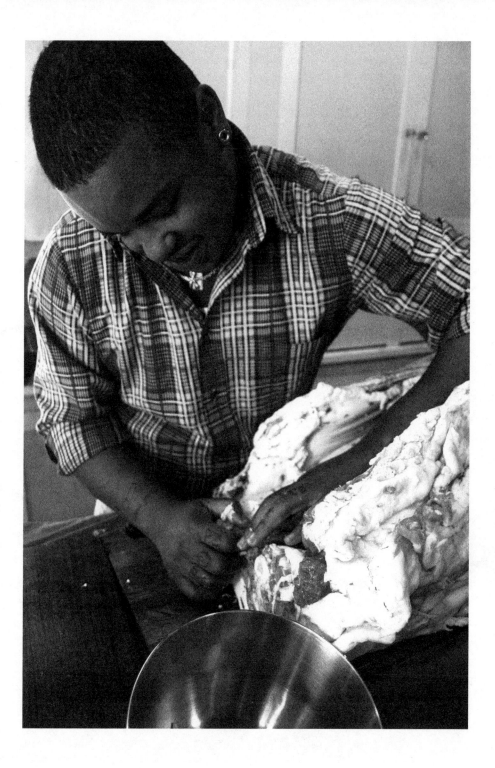

"Humble Beginnings" here.
The day The Ethical Butcher project came to
life scarcely hinted at the road I'd travel.
Heritage Farms Northwest, September 2009

Part Two

Why are you reading this book? Are you an omnivore looking to learn about better meat choices? A vegetarian hoping for a green light to start eating meat after twenty-two years of surviving on soy protein? A vegan looking for words to spark your latest blog? Are you sitting on the pescatarian fence, waiting for the nudge one way or the other? Still looking for the Ethical Shopper's Guide coded in these chapters?

Part Two points the mirror at you.

What do YOU believe about your food system? What is YOUR role in changing it? What do you know about where your meat comes from? How about your milk? Broccoli? Apples? Salmon? When people complain that good food is expensive, I don't argue with them. It is. But the reasons that good food is expensive, especially in the United States, are rarely examined. Responsible eating is a simple yet elusive equation for most of us. Consumers certainly carry a bulk of the weight. After all, YOU buy the food and YOUR body will eventually consume it and reap the risks or benefits of those foods. But the other side of the equation reaches far beyond personal responsibility. As a consumer, you can choose only from the selection that is offered to you. This is where corporations that produce food and government entities that are charged with keeping that supply safe come in. The next two chapters will explore each side of the equation as we look at the question of whether or not someone who wants to eat responsibly can eat meat and, more importantly, we expose the framework that forces you, the consumer, to CHOOSE between good and bad foods in the first place.

I don't want to tell you how to eat. I want to clear up all the confusing language and address a few misconceptions that will make your job easier. The following chapters ask you to delve deep into your own experiences and define yourself in this discussion. They will help you understand your food choices, the impact they make, and how to create a shopping list you can feel good about— and help you learn to argue down any food fascist who tries to make you feel bad about it.

5

The Abolitionist, the Pescatarian, and the Welfarist

The following excerpts come from a letter I received from "the Vegan Poet" in July 2010:

Listen carefully to the word "Butcher"

Someone who kills, takes the life of another being . . . a murderer.

I've been vegan for thirty-one years, and all my long-time vegan friends and I are living proof that we kill other feeling gentle animals NEEDLESSLY. We are living proof that you are taking their lives for no real reason . . . that is murder . . . and nothing ethical about it.

I say this in hopes of enlightening you, not to be mean.

The goal is to have everyone in the world to go vegan. To abolish animal slavery and exploitation (period).

I live by what is RIGHT . . . what is in Truth . . . and I don't follow the laws of man. . . I follow the laws of Love and Truth.

Those who live without exploiting other sentient beings ARE more evolved. I may believe myself to be of higher consciousness than you and the rest, but I won't harm you in any way. I will only try to lift your consciousness and enlighten you.

I wish for you and for everyone in the wonderful, the healthy and happy feeling of being vegan.

We all have the right to choose what we eat. The letter from the Vegan Poet in many ways underlines all the problems that relying on vegetarianism ignores. I love informed and open debate. I enjoy hearing impassioned arguments that defy my own reason. True solutions come only from working with, not against, those we see as "opposition." Real diversity means respecting people who don't share your beliefs, and I like to think that there's always something to learn from a different perspective. That said, I have learned to recognize when a debate has hit a moralist wall. Morals and deeply seated beliefs are not static or unchangeable, but they cannot be argued with. In fact, challenging someone's morals or beliefs is a ticket to defensiveness. Herein lies the problem with the debate on whether or not one can eat meat responsibly.

When asked, "Do you eat meat?," a veg will say no, but the reason behind the answer is just as important as the answer itself. We are all wrapped up in the wrong discussion, with horrible consequences. There are two debates: a moral and philosophical one about whether or not it is "right" to eat meat, and a practical one about whether or not one can eat meat responsibly. The former is a conversation that, like religion, is personal. Whether one abstains for moral reasons or practical ones, there is no right or wrong answer. It is a waste of time to argue with anyone about something so personal. I support everyone having the privilege to exercise their right to feed themselves and their families the foods they see as healthy. Thus I am only interested in the latter debate. We can't focus on whether people *should* eat meat or not when billions of people around the globe DO eat meat. That is a fact of most of human history and throughout most human civilizations. To debate over something so central to the human diet and centuries of culinary tradition is a frustrating diversion of energy that could instead be spent working on improving the standards that animals and humans encounter in the modern meat industry. Once I opened my eyes, I became entrenched in the drive to change the meat industry and its practices through my participation in the very world I had opposed for over a decade of my life. I wanted to serve meat that people could trust, and I did it. I wanted a direct relationship to the source, and I found it. I wanted ultimate accountability for a life-respecting death, and I found it. If you think it is inherently "wrong" to eat meat, there is nothing more to discuss. However, my internal debate was never a moral one; I never thought it was "wrong" to eat meat. I just thought all meat was poisonous stuff from disgusting corporations and there was no way around it. Once I realized that wasn't true, the rest was easy.

I've described my personal journey through vegetarianism, but the thinking behind the indulgence in or abhorrence of meat goes much further than my own experience. There is so much confusion about the meat industry, the health effects and benefits of animal products, and trendy dieting that people often don't even know why they make the food choices they do.

This chapter will examine many of the most common misconceptions and positions on the subject of meat eating. As you've probably guessed by now, nowhere in this book will you find a prescription for meat consumption. I will not tell people exactly what to eat; I'll only give the information people need to choose for themselves. In that, it is important to take stock of personal reasons for particular choices in advancing an ultimate goal of a healthier diet, a healthier relationship to food, and a healthier food system.

I have come to see three different approaches to the idea of eating meat. It is crucial that we decipher the varied goals of each. Separating moral arguments from pragmatic ones, over the next three sections, will help us get down to the meat of the matter.

Sins of the Abolitionist, or . . . Nice Vegans, This Is Not About You

Vegetarian abolitionists want absolute cessation of meat consumption on a wide, even global scale. They are convinced that all humans would benefit from a meat-free diet, and some, such as the Vegan Poet, are against all forms of human–animal symbiosis. I will say plainly that I find this position not as much flawed as problematic. It is perfectly fine to choose to abstain from animal products. It is a fact that most people eat far too much meat and would benefit from a plant-based diet. However, "plant-based" does not have to equal "meat-free," and it is a stretch of egotistical projection to assume that any one diet is appropriate for every single human on earth. This is a troublesome way of viewing others and is surely not based on any level of respect for the ability of others to make choices for themselves. Ironically, this assertion of the abolitionist's personal beliefs tramples upon the exercise of that right by others: everyone must bow to their dietary choices even as they devalue and dismiss the choices of others.

The abolitionist's numbers are dwindling as more and more people find ways to buy good meat and as more vegans relax into their less egomaniacal adulthood and realize that their decisions are just that, theirs. But there are still plenty of ornery herbivores out there ready to give you grief, and the Vegan Poet's letter put a spotlight on this mind-set. She clearly believes that she and her vegan brethren are better people—not *healthier* people, which would be a subjective term that I would leave alone. She believes they are genuinely more highly evolved creatures than those who eat meat. This moral superiority plagues the abolitionist set and places a divide between them and their ultimate goal of animal liberation. This superiority complex isn't about the animals in the system. It is about ego. Their dedication to an ideal blinds them to nuance and context. This kind of condescension smacks of colonialism. Big jump, huh? Not so much. By positing that ALL people should eat only one way, one erases thousands of years of culinary traditions of hundreds of cultures around the planet. Particularly when this idea is connected to ideas of "civilization" or "evolution," or when traditions and time-honored methods are seen as "primitive," there is a concerning context. North American colonizers kidnapped generations of First Nations people in the name of cultural assimilation and "progress." Food is culture. When we view the "other" as synonymous with "less than" or imply that others are uneducated, unhealthy, or in need of Western intervention, that is not progress—it is the legacy of colonization and classism. Abolitionists assume they have found The Truth and that it is their duty to proselytize to the "lower forms of life" still stuck in their flesh-eating phase. From this place of self-righteousness, they judge all others. When abolitionists use meat eating as a reason to disrespect, exclude, demean, or otherwise undermine the free will of another human, they prove themselves an ally to no one but their narrow-minded peers. This does nothing to change the living and dying conditions of animals in our food system. It only reassures and reinforces the abolitionist's convictions.

As one would expect, with a project called the Ethical Butcher and a vegetarian past, I've had more than my share of run-ins with rabid abolitionists. I find the level of irony in these interactions to reach heights of satire. I think my favorite will always be the vegan wearing brand-new Nikes who called me a "murderous bastard" in a Brooklyn bar a few years ago. Nike, of course, being a corporation with a well-documented record of sweatshop labor and human rights violations, this insult only made me laugh.

If the impetus was truly to liberate animals or improve their living conditions, these abolitionists would be less invested in their personal identities and much more concerned with moving forward toward the goal of a responsible food system that treats all with respect. Aside from the way abolitionists allow their personal liberties to supercede those of their fellow humans, the tunnel vision that drives them toward an end goal of global veganism stops them from seeing the full spectrum of solutions available to us. The abolitionist is tragically overinvested in personal morals and unnecessarily focused on meat and meat eaters as the problem. The abolitionist could instead be standing next to conscientious omnivores and honorable herbivores. The meat industry is supported by the oil, coal, and agriculture industries, which even an abolitionist is likely to continue supporting and even rely on heavily in daily life. The vegan in Nikes, the vegan in the SUV, the vegan who survives on a soy-based diet—he or she is no closer to ending the insufferable conditions for animals that are standard in the food industry. Turning one's back on the animals and humans within this system does not force change; it merely allows the abolitionist to disengage from the conflict and cling to his or her precious moral hierarchy. In the result of this turning away, omnivores are encouraged to persist in irresponsible meat consumption habits, and the meat industry is permitted to march on unchecked.

Cutting meat out of the "sustainable" or "healthy" eating conversation does a disservice to everyone working to change the meat industry and dismisses meat eaters from making healthy choices. Many assume that eating well means being a vegetarian. When people who sincerely want to change their habits hit the Vegan Wall, they are told that they are already pariahs, already lost causes, simply because they eat meat or animal products. Even when I was vegan and vegetarian, I took issue with natural food stores that didn't carry meat. What message does it send when people can't buy good meat in the same place they buy the rest of their health-giving food? It tells people point-blank: Meat Is Bad.

So these well-meaning shoppers buy their produce and bulk grains and then are kicked loose to scramble for their own sources of meat. On the contrary, every natural food store and farmer's market should be brimming with butchers cutting whole animals. Not just cured meats flown in from across the country—real butchers cutting whole animals from local pastures. Any store that bills itself as a farmer's co-op or natural food store or whatever other gimmicky label it chooses should be the face of change in the meat industry. If local farmers who raise good meat don't have a place in those establishments, where *do* they belong? How are customers supposed to find them to make better choices? These stores usually carry coffee, tea, chocolate, grapes, bananas, and other products with no compunction. The harvesting of each of these products has a long record of human rights violations and environmental destruction—yet we all agree that there are ways to continue consuming these products responsibly. What's the difference? Feelings. People have *feelings* about killing animals for meat. Even after all the questions of animal abuse, environmental damage, and health concerns are set aside, they are against meat consumption because they are fundamentally opposed to eating animals. This strong belief isn't a problem until it hinders others in their search for well-raised meats. Whether or not they choose to eat meat themselves, anyone who obstructs the efforts of others to raise, serve, and sell good, healthy meat has a lot more in common with the industry windbags than with those of us actually working toward change. To the extent that the abolition-ist has so influenced the market that stores and restaurants eschew meat from local farms in an effort not to offend this feisty constituency, any lag in the eventual wide-scale overhaul of our meat industry is on their heads.

Many of the plant-based proteins that human herbivores seek lean on industrial processes, creating foods in a way that is plain unhealthy for anyone. While meat is a food that we have been eating since quite early in our evolution as a species, soy sausage, "chikn" nuggets, and other mis-spelled mock meats are light-years away from meeting the rule of grandmotherly recognition. A whole foods diet can very well include meat and animal products, while man-ufactured meatless products have no place on that list. Generations of people around the globe have stretched the soybean to its natural extremes, providing a range of ways to eat this health-giving plant: edamame—or fresh soy-beans; *naturally processed* soy milk—the liquid of soaked and pressed soybeans; tofu—acid-activated pressed curds of soy milk; miso—fermented soy paste; tempeh—cut and fermented soybeans pressed into blocks; and many more obscure regional preparations. Yet when Western eyes set sight on this little bean, it was stretched beyond recogni-tion. Now, contrary to the flashy labels touting the health benefits of soy, the majority of soy products on the market are complete junk food.

The myriad ways of disguising soy in industrial foods are just as sneaky as the way that corn has shored up our food system—the two being the most commonly raised GMO crops in the world. The soy scheme is even more clever, though. Corn has been receiving the majority of the attention when it comes to the woes of our food system, but soy has become the darling of those concerned with sustainable foods. So while avoiding Evil Meat, people who eat these foods are fervently supporting Big Agriculture.

And that is a Big Problem.

Antimeat people go on about the amount of energy that goes into producing meat, but they fail to address a few points. First, our *entire* food system is in a tailspin. So even if you are a vegan raw foodist, unless you are raising everything yourself and living off the grid, you have a part in this too. To point to any one group as the sole cause of our food system woes is an injudiciously stunted action that we cannot afford. Our current food system depends on the large consumption of fossil fuels and mono crops; that is true whether you eat tofu or beef. Not to mention the energy it takes for a factory to turn beans into your precious soy amalgamate hot dog and to truck it from the factory in the Midwest to natural food stores all over the country, especially when one considers the overall carbon footprint of the companies responsible for producing and distributing these products. Many of the companies that manufacture alternative meat products are owned by large corporations that produce industrial meat products, and supporting these companies through your penchant for fake meat is indeed helping to keep real animals in the food system—ironically, to become what is essentially fake meat themselves due to the practices of the industry.

Let's face it, people go for fake meat and meatless versions of traditional meat dishes because meat is GOOD. It just is. We can all agree on that without agreeing that everyone should eat it. Some people also go for fake meat with the intention of filling presumed gaps in their nutritional intake, because veg folks are taught to be overly concerned with their consumption of a handful of nutrients. On that note, it is important to quickly discuss this obsession with protein, iron, and calcium, which is predominately due to advertising from the meat and dairy industries. It is true that animal-based foods are rich in these nutrients and provide more nutritional bang for your buck. However, according to the Centers for Disease Control, most humans over the age of fourteen need only forty-six to fifty-six grams of protein a day. If meat were to be your one and only protein source all day long, which it won't be since many foods provide protein, that's only about six ounces of meat. A nice big kale salad provides more calcium than a glass of milk. Iron can be found in many foods, and nutritionists have even narrowed down a list of "iron-inhibiting" foods that help support the body's natural iron retention abilities. The "Got Milk?" "Pork—the Other White Meat," "Beef—It's What's for Dinner," and other campaigns from the meat and dairy industries are successful attempts at convincing the public that we need these excesses. These ads tell us that we need what the industry supplies, copious amounts of meat and milk, but understanding your personal dietary needs will likely show that you need far less than you think. This truth can encourage most omnivores to eat less meat and dairy and most herbivores to chill out on replacements and supplements.

It's also important to note that any figure in common science invoked by abolitionists regarding meat is invariably based upon grain-fed animals and industrial production methods and is thus not transferable to animals raised on pastures and sold locally, as has been the custom for millennia. Meat has been a part of the human diet for much of our existence as a species. Anthropologists agree that *Homo sapiens* began as hunter-gatherers two hundred thousand years ago, having advanced from our previous scavenger role as *Homo erectus*. It is hunting for animals, in fact, that is credited with our evolution as a species in the endurance running hypothesis, a theory that states that persistent hunting of game was actually the evolutionary drive of the development of many human characteristics. The domestication of livestock defines our emergence into the Neolithic period, when humans began to farm and form societies about ten thousand years ago. Only very recently have studies begun to look at the benefits of raising and eating "sustainable" or "organic" meats. As these are just fancy labels for "HOW EVERYONE IN FUCKING HISTORY HAS DONE IT FOR—FUCKING—EVER," evolution, our histories, and worldwide culinary tradition tell us that raising and eating meat in traditional methods is

A-Okay. I don't need a lab coat to tell me that eating meat is normal and healthy, and neither does anyone else.

The fact that people look to these studies, and are so easily duped by propaganda, highlights our disconnect from traditional agriculture. A few generations ago, before industrial food took over, we wouldn't be having this conversation. If there were farmers in every community and farms surrounding every city, we would all know farmers firsthand. In the short spurts I've spent on farms around the country, I always came away with a better understanding of what it takes to raise food.

As a legacy of the industrial food system, most people, vegan or not, have never been to a farm or raised livestock. We have all been cheated out of the evolutionary wisdom that our ancestors took centuries to learn. This lack of knowledge informs some of the most outlandish beliefs and spurs on many campaigns that are actually detrimental to the improvement of standards in the meat industry. I have personally argued with vegans who are against castration of male animals—which is no different than spaying and neutering home pets, not to mention that large male animals such as bull steers, pigs, and roosters are aggressive and can inflict injury and even death to surrounding people and animals, as well as damage property. Anyone who has actually stood near a full-grown steer can imagine this. On farms and ranches, fencing helps protect species from one another, as well as from public roads and passersby, yet I've spoken to rabid abolitionists who contend that even fences are oppressive to livestock. These people have taken the sentient being argument to unnecessary lengths. As I've already stated, I will not engage in this argument because I do not believe it addresses the issues at hand. Yes, animals feel pain, form connections, and even possess alternate forms of intelligence, but in my book that does not mean they shouldn't be raised and killed for food. It means we owe them a good life and an honorable death.

Lastly, on this point, because the Vegan Poet invoked the abhorrent phrase *animal slavery*, I must speak to this egregiously offensive misnomer and other common empathetic trigger words. Let me be blunt: slavery is a violent human-to-human institution. Slavery is real, and only people are slaves. Animals have feelings, and some exercise free will, but to liken animal farming to slavery is emotional baiting. As a direct descendant of one of the most barbaric systems of slavery humanity has ever seen, I feel to compare the suffering of animals to that of my ancestors, or to the estimated twenty to thirty million humans in slavery around the globe today, is insulting and insensitive. These kinds of diminishing comparisons offend and disrespect millions of people. Many of those who throw this term around are likely benefiting from this human slavery in some way or another. I've similarly heard people call the meat industry an "animal gulag" and call meat a "Holocaust on your plate." I loathe any person who thinks it prudent to refer to killing animals for food with these terms. Put that sign down and join us on the ground, and you'll see that we do not need to compare the suffering of animals to that of humans to understand the gravity of the animal welfare situation in our food system. Comparing meat consumption to horrible crimes against humanity, and demonizing people for something so monumentally personal as a food choice, is far from helpful. It is oppressive in its repetition and perpetuation of capitalism's goals of ultimate assimilation. These disgusting references are scare tactics meant to demean and dehumanize. If you care about change, then change. It is important to identify and address the moral superiority complex that plagues so many herbivores and to give up on the unrealistic and elitist goal of worldwide vegan fascism.

Check Yourself, as They Say

The world is waiting for a better solution. Going vegan doesn't answer the bigger issues of a fossil-fuel-propelled world economy based on the abuse of humans, the destruction of the environment, and the unchecked rapacity of a few hundred people. Going vegan doesn't stop corporations from poisoning the earth and our bodies or keep the government from threatening the very choice to grow food for ourselves. Going vegan doesn't improve the labor camp living conditions of migrant workers who supply your precious veggies. Going vegan doesn't preserve generations of time-honored traditions, and it doesn't help us return to a more sustainable and enriching way of interacting with the earth. Most of all, going vegan does not absolve you from participation in the suffering of living beings or the destruction of our environment.

Going vegan makes YOU feel better. That's valid. We all want to feel better.

The Pescatarian Poacher

Now that the conversation has been started, we have to turn our attention to the guy slinking out the back door—you, rascally little pescatarian. I know, I know, none of this applies to you because you "only eat fish."

Proverbial bubble burst ahead: Whether you've taken the rather species-biased route of excusing the consumption of sea life while abstaining from land animals or you are genuinely under the impression that fish is a better choice, you are wrong. Salmon farms pollute rivers to make lox for your bagels, and countless species of marine animals are threatened with extinction thanks to the tuna that goes into your sushi roll.

As with the moral argument against eating meat, we must again appreciate that we are all able to decide what is "right" to eat. Fishing predates farming of land animals by over sixty thousand years. Millions of fishermen around the world, countless generations deep, rely on the sea for their wages. Entire cultures, cities, and cuisines are built around the fruits of the sea. It is not "wrong" to eat fish unless YOU feel it is wrong for YOU. It is also not "right" to eat fish because they are lower on the evolutionary chain.

We are humans; we are one of just a few of the 1.4 million known species that inhabit the top predator ring of the food chain. Our predecessors fought their way up here; don't begrudge them that recognition. Now that we've been up here a while, we have free choice of diet. This is something most other top predators don't share with humans. We get to choose what to eat, and we can eat a lot of different foods. Going vegan and drawing a line of demarcation among edible and inedible creatures are just a couple of choices in front of you. Choice is a beautiful thing, if you've got it. But, please, from the reading of this sentence forward, pescatarian, scrub the word *vegetarian* from your list of identifiers. You are either an eater of the Kingdom Animalia or not. Period. Such arbitrary criteria are pandering to a guilty conscience or wishy-washiness at best. Humans eat up and down Darwin's Lunch Line. There's no reason to pretend fish deserve to die more than pigs because they never grew legs.

Again, once we remove the moral weight of eating meat and take a pragmatic approach, the sustainability of the meat and fish industries are linked, but they are vastly different and completely separate. Each faces a similarly daunting but unique set of issues, and the pathway to responsible consumption of seafood is not the same as the road to good meat.

The international scientific community is unanimous

in its dire predictions for our sea life, particularly that affected by fisheries, yet the world marches on, filling its plates with endangered creatures ripped from the waves. The most commonly recited statistic on this topic is that at our current rates of fishing, we will have depleted the globe's fisheries by 2050. This line has been repeated in magazines and newspapers and on national news, but consumption continues at disgustingly ignorant levels.

According to the National Oceanic and Atmospheric Administration, only 5 percent of the ocean floor and a mere .5 percent of the oceans themselves have been explored. Still, a recent study shows that over 40 percent of our oceans are "highly affected" by human activity, while no area of the oceans remains unaffected. From pollution to commercial fishing to climate change, we have gotten our grubby little hands on every drop of water in the sea. The *World Register of Marine Species* states that we've discovered just a third of the world's 750,000 marine species. Yet we threaten nearly one thousand species with extinction, and 85 percent of the world's fisheries are now fully exploited or overexploited, or have collapsed. These sobering numbers are likely conservative estimates. Obviously, if we don't know how many species are in the oceans, there is really no way of knowing how many are already gone due to our actions.

One could write volumes on the complex conundrum of fish sustainability. I will try to concentrate mostly on the reasoning behind the mistaken ideas about fish eating, as well as issues that are unique to the fishing industry, as a means of helping you more clearly understand your options when it comes to the fishy side of eating. A brief look at several specific issues involved in both wild capture and aquaculture will only brush the surface. I could write a new guide to responsible seafood every month and still not get to all the pertinent information.

Thousands of species of sea life are transported around the world every day, pulled from waters on six continents and from every corner of the ocean. With 75 percent of the earth covered in water, the fish industry's impact on the global food system dwarfs that of the meat industry in environmental and ecological terms, if not economic ones. These are just some of the many elements that distinguish meat issues from fish issues.

One of the most important things to remember with fish sustainability is that we are talking about many, many species of animals. Every target species faces a unique set of challenges, and each target species affects a network of other sea life. This means that when you wonder whether or not a seafood choice is safe or responsible, you've got to be up to date on information pertaining to that specific species. Furthermore, you've got to be aware of where the fish came from in order to ascertain the sustainability of any given item; this is often the most difficult obstacle to overcome, as regulation of fisheries is a long-standing problem. Every country has varying levels of regulation of its fisheries, and many provide very little oversight at all.

While environmental destruction is involved in harvesting from both land and sea, the sea takes the brunt of the damage; even the runoff from industrial farms ends up in the ocean. With land animals, choosing responsibly is based on the way that people raise domesticated animals. With marine life, it's about the way we catch wild animals as well as the way we raise the species we farm. This difference both heightens the risks and complicates the solutions. A "bad" meat choice comes from a domesticated animal that has been mistreated and abused by humans and is full of hormones and corn. A "bad" fish choice is an endangered animal, caught by means that are causing the extinction of other species through environmental destruction or bycatch, an animal that is full of toxins and heavy metals, or one that is farmed in a way that threatens other species. In my estimation, it is easier to put a cow out to pasture on natural grasses and be nice to it before you kill it than it is to attempt to address the web of problems surrounding cod or tuna. With both farmed fish and wild fish presenting a separate set of problems, we will break them down and look at each individually. While I admittedly take a very conservative approach to my use and personal consumption of seafood, it is truly a matter of personal circumstance that should govern your food choices. There are many fisheries that are rebounding, or under proper management, and those can be great sources for seafood. Depending on where you live, locally caught fish can often be a delicious treat—count yourself lucky if this is an option. The farther from local sources of fish you live, the more your selection has to depend on imported fish. As soon as that local oversight is replaced by seafood from all around the globe, you are fishing in Pandora's Sea. Eighty-four percent of the seafood in the United States comes from imports with varying regulations.

Nowhere is this more apparent than with two of the most beleaguered species on our plates: shrimp and salmon. While cod, tuna, flounder, and many other target species have suffered considerably, these two stand above them in demand, much to their detriment. The issues are so complex and layered, and both salmon and shrimp are so popular among diners worldwide, that they are most important to consume responsibly, if at all.

How and where a fish is caught makes all the difference, and it is your job to do the legwork. You've got to question your fishmonger or server. To know what answers you are looking for, you must first understand the general terms and practices of the fish industry. Over the next few pages, we'll lay the line that leads to fish for dinner.

Problems with Wild Capture

Before getting into the practical information about capture methods, I want to point out a few more elements that are unique to wild fish. By "wild," I refer to fish and shellfish caught in our oceans, lakes, and rivers using anything from traps to fishing lines to large trawlers.

The two most astronomical problems facing our wild fish are *overfishing* and *bycatch*. Capture methods have allowed humans to completely deplete several stocks of fish and threaten many others. It is estimated that the global fishing fleet is twice the size needed to take every single fish out of the ocean at once. So I suppose any restraint should be applauded. When so many fish are caught on a long-term basis, the fish are unable to reproduce fast enough to keep up with the culling of their numbers. Eventually the balance tips too far in the favor of human technology, and that fishery, or species of fish, is considered "overfished," "fully exploited," or "depleted." North Atlantic cod, tuna, swordfish, and halibut fisheries have been limping along since the 1970s. This depletion of a target species spreads to other species in several ways. One is through "fishing down the web," or targeting the next best thing once the original species is gone. In this way, overfishing spreads through the entire marine ecosystem. This is shown in the way the fish market has responded to lower catches of top predators such as tuna and cod, which are long-lived and slow to reproduce and therefore vulnerable to overfishing, by turning to lower species on the web such as squid and crab, which reproduce in larger numbers in a shorter life span. Illegal fishing and poaching also account for a large portion of the overfishing problem; some experts put the share of unreported fish landings to be nearly one-fifth of the world's total catch. There is, as of yet, no universally accepted and enforced agreement regarding fishery standards. This makes it easy for poachers and lazy government regulations to guide the fish industry.

As the web of overfishing expands, so does the number of nontarget species, or bycatch. This issue is far more infectious, as it deconstructs entire ecosystems and brings the possibility of mass extinction by human hands to full fruition. While fisheries haul in unsustainable amounts of their primary or maybe even tertiary targets, they also pull in the sea's bounty, dead and dying. Sea turtles, sharks, marine mammals, and seabirds are all under threat from our fishing practices. In addition to those species, other fish—young fish of rebounding species undoubtedly—are also caught in the indiscriminate nets and hungry hooks. The shrimp industry is but 2 percent of the world's catch, but shrimp trawlers are said to discard 1.6 pounds of bycatch for every pound of shrimp, with the ratio even higher in some areas of the world. This industry accounts for more than one-third of the world's total bycatch.

To complicate the matter, fish move. As species migrate or swim through the waters under widely varied regulation, they move on and off the radar of responsible harvest. Swordfish are a great example of this and prove why committed decisiveness is required when choosing fish. In the 1990s, the Atlantic swordfish was in low number due to overfishing and poor management. Because large migratory fish such as tuna and swordfish move through waters governed by different countries, it takes coordination among several nations to enact any sort of effective strategy for halting the depletion of a species. Between 1999 and 2002, several international agreements calling for a 45 percent reduction in swordfish catches throughout the North and South Atlantic were reached. The U.S. National Marine Fisheries Service's enforcement of an off-limits swordfish nursery ground and strict regulation of the industry had resulted in a full recovery of the species by 2009. A horrible choice ten years ago, this fish is now considered a safer bet.

We are eating species into extinction. So many land animals are protected by regulation and by human sentimentality. Anyone who eats a tiger or panda bear would be seen as a poacher. Yet Chilean sea bass is on menus across the world. We can't eat domesticated animals into extinction. In fact, "conservation by consumption"—which will be discussed in the next chapter—relies on the eating of rare domesticated breeds to save them from extinction. This is different from eating fish because humans created these animals. By preserving a rare breed of pig, we are preserving human history and wisdom. Even if we allowed these heritage breeds to die off, we'd be affecting only human economies and the biodiversity of domesticated animals. Livestock are in an isolated food chain. Wild animals are not likely to die off if livestock does. However, with seafood, in a few more years you may be eating the last dolphin or bluefin tuna. That causes an imbalance that trickles down the entire marine food chain and into realms of biology humans haven't begun to comprehend. We are literally killing the ocean before we even get a chance to understand it. We cannot bounce back from that.

According to the National Marine Fisheries Service, about 80 percent of the seafood on the U.S. market is caught using trawlers, dredges, and purse seine nets, with an additional 8 percent coming from longlines and gill-nets. That means that almost 90 percent of the seafood on the market is caught using methods that carry significant risk to other marine species and that damage marine eco-systems. Using a dredge to fish for bottom dwellers is like using a bulldozer to hunt for rabbits. California fisher-ies harvest albacore tuna using only pole-and-line fishing or trolling; therefore they experience negligible bycatch compared to fisheries that catch tuna using purse seines, harpoons, or longlines. You must determine whether or not any wild fish is a good choice. It is an uphill battle, but worthy if you believe in the value of a healthy ocean for future generations. Frankly, for my money, a drastic reduction in wild captured seafood will be needed to see anything close to a full recovery in the world's fisheries.

Aside from all this, most wild fish contains some amount of carcinogenic toxins such as PCBs and heavy metals such as mercury. So, then, is fish farming, or aqua-culture, the answer? As one would assume based on our record with terrestrial agriculture, we haven't done such a good job.

Issues in Aquaculture

We've fished the oceans well over capacity. So it only follows that we'd find ways to raise fish ourselves, right? This would be a terrific solution if only we humans could stop ruining everything. Growth of fish farming has exploded exponentially as wild stocks are depleted. However, in a rush to fill a rapidly expanding gap between supply and demand, many aquaculture operations have resorted to cutting corners, putting wild fish at risk in several ways.

Many large carnivorous fish, such as tuna and salmon, require exhorbitant amounts of wild fish–based feed to grow. A salmon consumes about three times its weight in wild fish before it is harvested. Some fish farms intentionally catch juvenile wild specimens and raise them to market size in open nets in the ocean in a practice called sea ranching. Most eel on the market is produced this way, causing numbers of wild eel to plummet. The demand of these fish farms puts an even heavier demand on the already waning wild fish catch, with more than a quarter of the annual wild catch going to aquaculture. This is no small figure.

Fish farms can negatively impact the environment both through pollution and habitat destruction. Aquaculture is credited with 50 percent of the loss of the world's mangrove trees, with the majority of that damage caused by shrimp farms that have sprung up in clear-cut mangrove stands in Asia. Pollution from fish farms happens in a few different ways but always entails the release of feces, chemical treatments, excess feed, and medications introduced to captive fish. These substances are allowed to escape from farms that are set up in open water, as is the case with many salmon and shrimp farms. Depending on currents, this pollution may be carried away and dispersed in surrounding waters, or it may simply settle, literally burying the seafloor in feet of fish crap. Either way, these farms are putting the oceans and native species at risk of infection and death due to contact with these substances.

These aren't the only escapees that put a bad name on aquaculture. Nonnative and genetically modified fish species that escape threaten neighboring native species— many of them already under threat, or recovering, from wild capture methods. These fish escape and interact with native species through competition for habitat, disruption of precious spawning grounds, and spread of disease. Genetically modified salmon have also begun to mate with, and replace, native species of salmon throughout the Atlantic. This dilution of native genetic lines is seen as a negative factor in the survival of already vulnerable salmon runs. GMO salmon also prey upon wild fish and form feral populations, completely altering the local ecosystem of any given body of water. The global dispersement of tilapia is an example of this issue. After increased production of this fish as a replacement for depleted cod stocks over the last sixty years, we now see feral populations of tilapia in over ninety countries in every warm-water habitat. Because we don't yet fully understand the oceans, we cannot fully appreciate the long-term implications of these disturbances. As long as open pens and nets are in operation, these factors will continue to be a threat. While they present isssues on the energy front, enclosed systems are taking ground throughout the industry and offer a solution to some of the biggest problems found with open systems.

You see, it's a bit of a "damned if you do, damned if you don't" sort of situation. Both wild and farmed fish present a list of very real issues that must be considered before you order your next fish and chips. Several species of farmed fish are better choices than their wild counterparts, and as we will very likely continue to overfish our oceans, the next few decades will see a definite slow and steady lean into farmed fish as the only source. Supporting the right operations while the industry is still developing will dictate whether this replacement of industry is a good or bad thing. If done well, and coordinated with responsible wild capture methods and effective regulation of wild fisheries, aquaculture could give wild fish a few decades to recover. So maybe I won't be able to serve my kids fish, but there will be fish for their grandkids. I feel good about that.

Why You Should Pretty Much Stop Eating Shrimp and Salmon, or . . . BUMMER ALERT

No one wants to hear this, but it has to be said: We MUST stop eating shrimp and salmon. Now. Today. Hell, last week. I know, I know. You LOVE shrimp and your health-focused diet tells you to eat a six-ounce piece of salmon every damned day. Well, guess what? Your healthy choices are causing the destruction of the environment and extinction of countless species of plants and animals.

Farmed and wild-caught shrimp and salmon both have a staggering laundry list of bad traits. Because they are so valuable on the international market, changes in both industries are sluggish. Responsible farming could alleviate pressure on their wild counterparts, but both shrimp and salmon aquaculture carry many of their own risks. It will take a drastically reduced demand on both the farms and wild catch to see a better reality for these two beloved and tasty sea creatures. Start expanding your palate, pescatarian. The following information will help you to choose the best option for your next dinner.

SHRIMP SUCKS! Why You Shouldn't Eat Most WILD Shrimp

Bycatch and Discards

Shrimp fisheries employ trawlers, or very large nets, that scoop up everything in their path. Worldwide, the shrimp industry is blamed for consistently having the highest rates of bycatch, nontarget species, and discards— unwanted catch that is simply thrown back into the sea. The average ratio of discard to shrimp can be a much as six to one. In the Gulf of Mexico, four and a half pounds of crabs and fish are caught for every pound of shrimp hauled in. According to the Worldwide Fund for Nature, shrimpers in the Gulf of Thailand throw fourteen pounds of bycatch overboard for every pound of shrimp. Many of the animals caught in these nets are critically endangered sea turtles.

Habitat Damage

Shrimp trawlers drag nets along the seafloor, killing and collecting everything they encounter. While it is officially up for debate, shrimp from the Gulf of Mexico have also exhibited signs of contamination from oil and dispersants from the 2010 BP oil spill.

Why You Shouldn't Eat Most FARMED Shrimp

Destroyed Mangroves

Many shrimp farms are located in once flourishing mangrove forests, which provide a unique habitat to many species in Asia. These forests also provide traditional fishing grounds for locals. Removing this valuable habitat thus affects local populations. Continuing to purchase farmed shrimp encourages farmers to repeat the destruction.

Pollution

A poorly managed shrimp farm bears a striking resemblance to a feedlot. Thousands of shrimp live in their feces and are therefore treated with pesticides and antibiotics to combat the unsanitary conditions. Many farms also allow untreated contaminated water to flow into the environment.

Dependence on Wild Fish

For every ton of farmed shrimp, 1.4 tons of wild fish are needed as feedstock. Destruction of mangroves for shrimp farms also puts wild fish at risk. Finally, shrimp can carry exotic diseases that enter local waters and affect native species.

What Kind of Shrimp You Should Look For

Trap-caught wild shrimp from British Columbia and other West Coast waters is a good option because the traps target only shrimp and when used correctly cause minimal damage to the seafloor. Wild small seasonal catches of East Coast shrimp can be found from Florida, Maine, and eastern Canadian provinces. If the shrimp isn't trap caught, it isn't a good choice. It is so difficult to track down the origin of imported shrimp that it is better to avoid any shrimp of unknown provenance.

What's Wrong with Eating WILD Salmon?

Severely Depleted or Fully Exploited Stocks

Most of the world's stock of salmon is either near extinction or severely depleted. Atlantic salmon have been nearly

decimated, with just 1 percent of their historic population swimming a few rivers of Maine. Pacific salmon are
threatened in the West, with states closing more salmon
fisheries each year or placing very low quotas on fisher-
man to protect rebuilding populations. We have attacked
this majestic fish from both ends by overfishing and by
cutting them off from spawning grounds, thus lowering
their birthrates and reducing their ability to bulk up their
numbers.

Very Few Viable Fisheries Available Worldwide

Alaska's well-managed fisheries produce nearly all the
wild salmon for the world. While salmon fisheries from
California to British Columbia have seen devastating
losses in their catches, over the last twenty years Alaska
has maintained catch levels that exceed all other western
fisheries combined. This makes Alaskan salmon the best
choice for wild salmon. But it also places a world of
weight on a few fisheries. By turning your tastes toward
other options, you can take a part in assuring that these
fish continue to rebound.

What about Eating FARMED Salmon?

Pollution

Salmon farms are known to cause a lot of waste, and all
that waste has to go somewhere. Feces, antibiotics, pesticides, and other chemicals travel from the farm into the

surrounding waters in commonly used open systems that allow water from farms to be released into the open sea or rivers.

Escapes

Salmon that escape from farms interbreed with and out-compete native species, making the recovery of native wild salmon species more difficult.

Disease

Diseases run rampant in the overpacked facilities of many salmon farms, where fish swim in a sea of their own excrement. Sea lice and salmon anemia are two pathogens that thrive in this environment. The possibility of disease and unsanitary conditions necessitate the use of chemical agents such as antifoulants and disinfectants—all of which end up in your body and the surrounding waters. Escaped farmed fish also introduce disease to native populations.

Dependence on Wild Fish

Farmed salmon require three times their weight in wild fish and fish oil. Because you are ingesting triple the amount of wild fish, this defeats the purpose of choosing farmed fish over wild in the interest of the environment.

GMO Salmon

FDA-approved GMO salmon is set to hit the market without so much as a label to allow consumers to avoid it. The long-term risks of manufacturing living beings for food has obvious ethical implications. It also encourages us to continue other unsustainable practices in defiance of the need to rein in our actions across the board.

What Are Good Alternatives to Salmon?

Most notably, arctic char, a cousin of salmon, has been successfully farmed in closed tanks for several years and offers a much more desirable alternative to both farmed and wild salmon. It has a similar flavor and texture to salmon and is even easier on the wallet because, well, you aren't eating a FREAKING FRACKING ENDANGERED ANIMAL. Easy switch.

It's Up to Us

Local, seasonal fish is always a better option, and lowering our overall consumption of seafood relieves some of the pressure on our oceans. While it is up to individual consumers to make better choices, it is also the responsibility of chefs and fishmongers to change their own buying habits and educate customers. Just as the industry has to stop bending to uneducated and inconsiderate consumer demand, so too must we be unapologetic in our stringent sourcing standards. I've seen too many shops and restaurants that implement grading systems to help customers yet continue to stock the most highly threatened items. Why institute a green, yellow, and red grading system to rate the sustainability of your products and then offer the red, or most destructive, items?

Those red items have to become off-limits. It is the duty of the chef or fishmonger to explain why the menu is changing or why a customer's favorite selection is no longer available. We must all consider ourselves guardians and stewards of the ocean. If we don't start making these hard choices now, and help our customers understand the impact of these choices, we are furthering the disaster in our seas.

Check out some of the resources for sustainable fish listed below. Many of them offer digital guides that can be installed on smart phones for the most up-to-date information. Pocket guides and comprehensive websites are other great ways to find out about the fish you are thinking of eating.

Resources for Information
on Seafood Sustainability

Monterey Bay Aquarium:	*montereybayaquarium.org*
FishWise:	*fishwise.org*
Blue Ocean Institute:	*blueocean.org*
Sustainable Fisheries Partnership:	*sustainablefish.org*
Ocean Conservancy:	*oceanconservancy.org*
FishChoice:	*fishchoice.com*
Environmental Defense Fund:	*edf.org*
Marine Stewardship Council:	*msc.org*

The Winningest Welfarist

I didn't do all that bubble bursting to leave you deflated, my friends. We just needed to clean house a bit. Now we can start talking about what responsible consumption really looks like. Whether you choose to eat meat or not, everyone should strive to be conscientious consumers and winning welfarists. We must all be concerned with the overall health of our entire food system, as well as that of our local communities. If you are enjoying a grass-fed steak while your neighbor tries to figure out how to make one Tyson chicken breast feed four people, you are complicit in the inequality that plagues our culture and the continuation of our broken food system. As that system relies on a class divide when it comes to access to good food, with an eye toward feeding whole communities, there are many ways conscientious eaters can help spread healthy habits past their own kitchens. Some of these ideas will be discussed over the final chapters of this book, but many of them are for you to create yourself.

This may be the closest I get to a "How to Eat Meat" guide in this entire book, but keep in mind that it is up to you to decide what eating responsibly means. These are just guidelines that I've found helpful in my experience. I invite everyone to reconceptualize and refine this list to fit their local circumstances. Maybe you are a hunter in Montana and eat only meat that you hunt—AWESOME. Most of these rules wouldn't apply to you. On the other hand, if you live somewhere like Phoenix or Las Vegas and rely mostly on imported foods, you may need to be a little more conservative to consistently make good choices. Save the lobster dinner for your trip to Maine.

The Winningest Welfarist . . .

. . . eats a PLANT-BASED diet with minimal to no animal products. Surprise, surprise. After a few years in the meat biz, the ex-vegan butcher says, "Eat Less Meat." Though I've been asked repeatedly to state a recommended frequency of meat eating, I can't prescribe a diet for anyone but myself. I know how much meat and dairy work for my body. Learning to listen to your body is a personal journey and one some of you may not be ready to undertake. However, the signs can often be loud and clear. If you are having diet-related health issues, you already know that meat, dairy, and processed foods are likely to blame. Numerous studies and common sense tell us that a diet high in whole, natural, and minimally processed plant-based foods is healthy for most bodies. People can surely be welfarists regardless of their standing on the consumption of meat as long as they respect others as they choose for themselves. If they do choose to eat animal products, they buy the best they can find and afford. They are most austere in their consumption of seafood.

Recalling the low amount of protein that most people need daily, equal to just six ounces of meat or a few servings of dairy and eggs, and considering that protein can be found in many, many foods, you need less meat and dairy than most people think. A three-ounce portion of meat fills nearly half of an average adult's daily demand for protein. That sounds like just a bite to many Americans, but this is how humans have eaten meat for all of our history. While it is an adjustment to move away from a diet based on animal products, once your body adjusts to the lower amounts of cholesterol, fats, and protein (which are acids and which in high amounts affect blood chemistry) and the increased amounts of fiber from plant foods, you are not likely to regret your transition.

Meat has always been scarce and special. The modern illusion of plenty created by a meat industry that churns out meat 365 days a year comes at a high cost. Respecting the natural limits of our gut will lead to a respect for the natural limits of traditional farming. When you eat meat only once or twice a week, or even once a month, not only will you find that you can afford a nice, high-quality rib eye or pork chop, you will also see that hunk of meat for the treasure that it is. I'd sure rather eat a gorgeous roasted duck from a local farm once a year than eat a McDonald's hamburger every day. Wouldn't you?

The Winningest Welfarist . . .

. . . seeks the smallest impact on the environment and pushes for positive changes in the industry. Welfarists are driven to seek ever-improving standards in the food industry and to be aware of their own personal impact on the industry and the environment. They recognize their power and their responsibility when it comes to "voting with their dollars." Welfarists, not abolitionists, are to thank for advancements in the humane treatment of animals in the food industry. Make no mistake: big business responds only when there's money to be made. When the egg industry saw that people would pay more for eggs from chickens that weren't kept in cramped, shared battery cages, it began to provide eggs from cage-free and free-roaming chickens. Grass-fed beef has exploded in popularity because people are willing to pay more for steer that aren't wading through excrement and being poisoned with subsidized corn. Similarly, a kibosh on swordfish from chefs and buyers over just a few short years allowed a full recovery of that species. The welfarist recognizes his or her role in the push for a better food system and takes it seriously. Progression is infinite. The goal is not chickens that are free from cages but never step foot outside a cement warehouse. Welfarists will keep pushing until free-moving animals eating the diets nature intended for them are the standard and not the exception.

Welfarists also make choices that improve the living standards of their fellow humans as well. Improving wide-scale access to good food benefits everyone; having a high-priced farmer's market in an affluent area of town does nowhere near the good that having one in every neighborhood does. Welfarists support fair labor practices by shopping at co-ops and other community-based businesses.

The Winningest Welfarist . . .

. . . is interested in staying connected to sources of both animal- and plant-based foods. Welfarists have an interest in feeding themselves and in investing in that process mentally, financially, and physically. Whole animal butchery takes time. If I wanted to speed things up, I could surely order packaged cuts. But because I am dedicated to the traditional method of butchery, I gladly take the extra labor and time to cut the meat by hand. In the same way, the welfarist must prioritize high-quality foods and be willing to work to find them. The American food industry relies on your being "too busy" to eat well. That's capitalist brainwashing bullshit. The hidden message is: "Eat this vitamin-fortified junk and get back to work." The brazen welfarist flips the machine the bird and starts a community garden on an NYC rooftop. Welfarists smuggle raw milk to their friends and organize CSAs in poor neighborhoods. They teach their friends and coworkers how to make their own bread, preserves, and salami.

Respecting the seasonality of both fauna and flora, the welfarist honors the natural cycles of the earth. People are just starting to grasp the fact that strawberries in June taste better than strawberries in January, but most people are nowhere near comprehending the seasonal availability of salmon or pork. Just think about it: grass-fed beef comes from cattle that graze naturally on open pasture. Wild salmon are fish caught on their annual spawning runs. These are by definition seasonal items. If we are truly committed to changing our habits, seeing items like these as rare delicacies is a natural next step. Just as nature provides a selection of produce for every season of the year, so too can we find seasonal sources of meat. The trick with both is being open to experimentation and not being attached to one item. From eating a wider variety of animals to eating a wider variety of produce, the welfarist is always ready for what Mother Nature is serving.

The Winningest Welfarist . . .

. . . respects all life and is not arbitrary or wasteful in consumption of animal products.

All life is sacred. It doesn't matter if I want to eat lamb, iguana, dog, steer, or tuna. Life is life, and none of those animals is more or less deserving of my fork. Unlike the pescatarian deeming fish as deserving of death for food simply because they are fish, the welfarist is not hung up on sentimental and arbitrary lines that drive food choices. Whether I want to eat a bunny or a crab, the action of taking life is the same and should be respected as such. Cuisines all over the world have made use of every imaginable source for the power pack of nutrients that animal products provide. Humans eat animals ranging from ants and grubs to caribou. And until the industrial meat system took over, humans also ate most or all parts of the animals they killed for food.

Pigs are not made of bacon and pork chops; fish have heads and tails full of delicious meat; and cows are not burgers on legs. If you eat animals, *eat animals.* Expand your palate, try other parts of the animal, and experiment with new cuts and techniques. The closer we get to returning to a whole animal system, the better off we will be. Widening your selection to other parts of your favorite animal may provide an opportunity to buy more or higher-quality meat. If you have your heart set on a local, heritage breed pork loin roast and that's out of budget, check out the prices on shoulder roasts and impress your guests just the same. Instead of wasting money buying boneless, skinless, tasteless chicken breasts, buy a whole bird for the same price. Incidentally, this change is of particular importance because it is the demand for these large breasts that has driven so much of the horrid genetic manipulation of industrial-breed chickens over the last couple of decades. Taste is another consideration. It is not imperative that we all like the same flavors. If you are into the strong flavors of offal (organs), they can provide even higher amounts of valuable nutrients than prime cuts at a fraction of the cost. Since organs such as the kidneys and liver cleanse the blood and must be eaten soon after slaughter, it is wise to limit the eating of offal to very fresh, local, and chemical-free animals. This is a never-ending exploration, but be brave and keep trying new things. Even if chicken hearts aren't your thing, you may find scrambled goat brains to be your favorite breakfast.

Aside from the nutritional and practical reasons for eating more of each animal, it is just plain disrespectful to waste and disregard parts of the animal that you've deemed wrong or disgusting. I don't *love* tripe, but to act like it is law that man shall not eat the organs of the beast would be sacrilege. I remember my first beef heart burger in Portland a couple of years ago. If you haven't had one before, know that a beef heart burger is the meatiest, richest beef burger you can find. It's full of lean muscle. Cooked up to medium-rare, it's just bloody heaven. Cows have hearts. They taste good and are good for you.

Get over it. The meat-eating welfarist is an adventurous omnivore.

There's no natural law that states that humans can eat only beef, pork, and chicken. We all know that. So the welfarist has an open palate and open mind when it comes to trying new meats. Moving past the American meat trifecta, we have less common livestock such as lambs, rabbits, goats, and turkeys. These industries don't produce at the same capacity as the Great Trio; the animals are often raised with higher standards as a matter of course and can be good options—though it is still wise to check out sources and stick to local farms as much as possible. Then there's wild game—this is where the fun begins. Outside of personal taste and personal moral or religious objection, the only rules when choosing whether or not it is good to eat any given species of wild animal are: Is this animal endangered? How did it get to my plate? As long as the animal isn't rare and was caught in a way that didn't cause undue harm to other animals, people, or the environment, you're golden.

The Winningest Welfarist . . .

. . . stays educated and is more concerned with verifiable standards than labels.

Welfarists will select the highest quality of meat and fish available based on individual circumstances. They follow the news and are invested in their local food communities.

They support local farmers through direct relationships instead of relying on flashy labels and "Friendly Farmer" advertising. They do not pledge lifelong allegiance to any one source; they are vigilant in keeping abreast of the ever-changing practices of their sources. Farms are businesses, and businesses grow. Sometimes a farm that used to raise pigs for the local farmer's markets starts shipping pork all over the country. If welfarists aren't aware of changes at a beloved farm, they could find that they've been buying from Big Ag in disguise. Welfarists do not depend solely on labels from the government or third-party organizations. They do their homework and find out what all the jargon is really saying.

This is where responsibility moves from consumer to producers and industry. I say, "It's up to us," but really, personal responsibility goes only so far. The industry chooses what to produce as well as how to market or sell items to consumers. Navigating this manipulation can be a difficult task. The next chapter will break down a lot of the misconceptions about those presumably trustworthy labels.

ᥩ ᥩ ᥩ

Making the best food choices you can is all it takes to be a responsible eater. No one diet or eating style fits everyone in all situations in all regions. That would be too easy and too boring. No, the conscientious consumer is engaged in and educated about the food system and makes decisions based on a balance of issues that are relevant to him or her each and every day. The conscientious consumer lives a dynamic life involving exciting new foods and food projects and is interested in supporting an overall return to traditional and more sustainable practices. A return to traditional methods and sustainable practices includes raising animals, eating meat, and eating animal products. Butchers are a key component in that transition as intermediaries between farmers and consumers. While consumers must do their part by buying and eating more responsibly produced foods, chefs, butchers, fishmongers, and grocers carry a brunt of the weight. We must make better choices and lead the way. The industry won't change unless we do. Sure, this might be a losing battle. We are fighting a monster of a machine, but we can find kinks in its armor. I jumped into the game of meat because I wanted to see it drastically changed, but I have no intention of beating Big Ag at its own game. I want to call foul and stop the clock indefinitely. I want Tyson, Monsanto, Smithfield, ConAgra, and many other corporate "people" to be ejected from the playing field altogether.

But where's the ref when you need him? That is the supposed duty of the USDA and FDA, right? They are charged with keeping our food supply safe and healthy. Yet these torturous, filthy slaughterhouses and factory farms operate under their supervision, and these agencies brazenly approve the cancerous spread of genetically modified foods. I can't legally buy a sumptuous raw milk cheese from a farm upstate, but I can surely buy beef from cows that lived waist-deep in their own feces? And in the same day an agency gives a passing grade to that cesspool of beef (barely) on legs, it wants to go to the small farmer down the road and tell him how to grow beef organically?

The game is rigged. The next chapter is the closest I can come to a game plan.

6

The Green Fog

There are many tools that people turn to in hopes of wading through confusing and often contradictory information about the dangers and benefits of certain foods. But by submitting to dietary dogmatism, we let our own internal compasses rust, losing our way to finding real food rules that work for us. Much the same way that filtering through the real meanings, incentives, and consequences of vegetarianism and other blanket restrictions on our eating habits helps us decide what foods we want to eat, we must likewise use our most critical eyes as we take a deeper look at what all the labels mean when we walk through the aisles of our grocery stores.

When I left my vegetarian days behind me, I finally began to weigh each individual food choice based fully on its merits, not on what food group it fit into. We have to think about a lot more than whether our burgers are made of soy, beef, or turkey. What about where that soy, beef, or turkey comes from? Most of what we've been taught to look for by the meat industry, as well as by mainstream culture, depends heavily on labels, both literal and figurative. This is a given when nearly everything we buy is packaged, transported, scanned, and processed through corporate and government channels. Deconstruction of these labels leads to a clearer view of both the culinary quality and the sustainability of our food. For too long the battle has been too focused on a specific diet: vegan versus low fat versus raw versus local. The genuine enemy is the entire system of government-supported industrial food.

While farmers, chefs, butchers, and a more informed and concerned public demand sustainable products from sources they can trust, the fact is many must find creative ways to circumvent regulations that are ostensibly for our protection. As I travel, documenting and working with people behind this shift in the industry, I am often struck with awe at the degree to which people must fight to bring good food to our tables. Striking out against government regulations, turning down farm subsidies and agribusiness, farms take many risks in stepping outside of the mainstream industry. It is perfectly legal to carry an assault rifle, but raw milk enthusiasts are forced to buy and sell milk on the black market. Farmers of pasture-raised animals struggle to get their meat to one of a few

USDA slaughterhouses around the country, lucky to find one that doesn't abuse its workers. Due to the concentration of meat processing plants in our country, often they do this risking contamination from the factory farms that send their meat to be processed at the same plants. Then, right next to so-called artisanal producers who have glossy shops and flashy logos, they vie for customers at farmer's markets and cross their fingers that they make even a nominal profit. Chefs and butchers who want to go directly to the source for their meats are restricted by USDA regulations that undervalue traditional practices while thousands of steer stand up to their knees in waste in fully licensed concentrated animal feeding operations. We've all seen the film clips and photographs. We have to start wondering why this system continues and look at the ways the USDA chooses to use its regulatory powers. Often, of course, the agency penalizes small farmers and small producers. We must turn to our government and demand protection not from the small chance of a microbe in a glass of local raw milk but from the concrete risk of infection from food processing plants that operate through years of violations.

Today, small farms and home cooks are picking battles with the USDA. REAL butchers, the ones who saw off heads and snap leg tendons, are teaching people how to find and use better meat. Restaurants and stores across the continent that pay more than lip service to "sourcing locally" are throwing out the excuses and proving their intentions. All the while, as this unflagging work goes on, corporations and government entities have both found ways to repurpose any terms they can and to purchase any label they can't. "Going green" is just a trend to these companies, not a true evolution of policy. Nearly every "natural" product on the shelves of the grocery store is manufactured by a large, old-school Big Food business that continues to behave irresponsibly through the majority of its actions. New buzzwords are thrown around constantly as honest growers and producers try to distinguish their foods from these imitations. Just as quickly as a word pops up, the industry finds a way to apply that pristine label to its own dirty practices. Pearls on swine. The drive for industrial animal agriculture to manipulate rhetoric is the same drive the USDA has for manipulating the very language that used to describe food created with integrity. I call this manipulation and culture of misrepresentation the Green Fog because it is quite successful in clouding judgment and making good choices a murky endeavor. This chapter will lay out everything you need to burn through the Green Fog on your way to good, honest food.

The Green Market

Before industrial foods existed, before the processing plants and distribution centers and food technology labs, food was just food: real ingredients, bound to laws of nature. Industrial food came about as a solution to the woes of traditional production methods. Diseases, pests, slow growth rates, spoilage, inconsistencies, fragility in transport—all of these were the targets of the industrialization of our food system. We sped up the time it takes to bring animals to slaughter. We made foods that can sit for years without rotting and seeds that are impenetrable to most pests. We transport food around the globe to keep any idea of scarcity or low yields far from mind. We made big strides. We just went too far. Now we live in a world where most people have never grown so much as a tomato for themselves, would prefer a ninety-six ounce Big Gulp of colored corn syrup to a glass of water, and think it's "gross" to talk about where your meat comes from.

As a reaction to the mainstream industry of corn-based, chemical-laden foods in the marketplace, the last few decades have seen a steady increase in companies making natural foods and consumers seeking out those foods. This "natural foods" industry is now worth over $91 billion according to an annual overview by *Natural Foods Merchandiser*. An industry opposed to many mainstream practices, natural foods businesses have been instrumental in improving standards of the food industry as a whole. Companies that used to get away with pumping foods full of chemicals have begun scrambling to figure out how to make foods that can actually be considered "real."

Marketing tactics that twist the merits of industrial products have been one way the mainstream food industry has competed with natural foods. Another way is through usurping the very techniques and language that set natural foods apart from their industrial counterparts. Yet another is through the acquisition of natural brands by industrial ones.

It is a slippery slope to try to fit traditional methods and practices into an industrial context. The two systems are by definition mutually exclusive, and striking a balance between the two is an elusive feat for all of us in the food industry. We cannot allow the natural foods industry to follow the same path that industrial food has. These corporations are hip to what you are looking for. They are putting farmers on their packages, and nearly every commercial brand has a "natural" or "organic" line. We need to be a little more skeptical of this trend. All that glitters isn't gold—or good for you.

The mainstream food industry has attempted, with some success, to co-opt the green foods movement. Many people are gung-ho about Walmart being the number-one purchaser of organic foods. I wonder how thrilled those shoppers are about the many class-action lawsuits that have been brought against the company or the recent labor strikes in Walmart's warehouses in twelve states, where workers picketed for the first time in the company's fifty-year history of crushing union-organizing efforts by employees. I personally am pretty stoked about the latter. McDonald's hopes you swoon over ads of rugged Idaho farmers who raise its potatoes, and Heinz wants you to know exactly what goes into its ketchup because it uses its very own special tomato. What both companies fail to mention in their glowy ads is that both of these are GMO crops. They are banking on you falling for these ploys in your hunt for more trustworthy sources of food. They use these tactics because they've caught on to the fact that many people are looking for a connection to their food. But if that's what you are looking for, these corporations have no place in that equation. Local means local. Truly shopping local allows you to ask all the questions you want—without the glossy ad, sprouting sunflowers, or harp music.

NO, local won't feed the world. It isn't supposed to. NO, seasonal foods won't fill markets to the brim year-round in every climate. But the industrial food system hasn't solved the world hunger crisis either. We would be naive to believe the industry's claim that this level of production is about feeding the world. Consistent with the boasting on the McDonald's website about being the number-one purchaser of beef in the United States, most of the meat produced in our food system is destined directly for fast-food chains and processors of value-added foods. Grains are raised to a surplus at falsely reduced costs through government subsidies and then fed to cows to supply ground beef for McDonald's and pumped into thousands of "food" products. All the while, some of this cheap grain is also exported around the globe, driving down prices of grain in other countries and putting overseas farmers out of work, thus removing not only nations' ability to grow food for themselves but also their ability to buy the grains we export to them. In many regions, war, much of it over oil, cuts off access to foods, as does environmental damage from industrial practices. So while the industry sits back and says this is the only way to feed the masses, I say they are the only ones capable of killing them all. I'm not buying what they are selling, and neither should you.

Our top goal in dispelling or conquering the Green Fog should be as little participation in the industrial system as possible. It is nearly impossible for most people to step very far from the grid, but even small changes can make a world of difference. The important key is keeping this goal in mind and continuing to make progress in your journey toward defining a healthy lifestyle. Working toward that goal makes the corporate food industry increasingly irrelevant to your life. The more you depend on the local farmer's market for produce, the less your salad depends on mono crops and Big Ag. Local sourcing is not a chore; it is a gift and a tool for separation from industrial methods and their destructive processes. That will mean searching for local sources of meat and dairy and also produce, grains, and other products. The meat will be fresher and easier to examine for practices you support. While unpredictable, the produce you'll find at local markets will likely be more flavorful and fresher than the widely distributed, gas-ripened versions in the chain grocer. Your homemade granola will not only taste better than the boxed variety but it will be cheaper too. All this talk just keeps going back to the same ideas that have sustained humanity for millennia: Make and grow your own food or trade services and money directly with those who do. You don't want to hear it. I don't want to say keep saying it. But it's the answer.

So long as we are dependent on a system that widely distributes commoditized, "dependable" brands and a comfortably monotonous selection of foodstuffs, we are being led into a world where a handful of companies run every facet of our lives. It is not a coincidence that four companies own over 80 percent of the meat industry and six companies own over 90 percent of the media. There's a common misconception that eating well has to take longer and be more expensive. The corporate food industry tells us that efficiency, consistency, and conformity are to be prized over time-honored tradition, excellence, masterful skill, individuality, and quality. When you walk into a grocer in January and decide that those pale, chemically treated tomatoes and flaccid asparagus are more desirable than the healthfully varied and unpredictable bounty of root vegetables of that season, you are agreeing with this assertion. By accepting without question the commoditized products foisted upon us, we are effectively turning to these abusive, greedy corporations and saying, "Thank you, Sir. May I have another?"

Say I want to make sandwiches every day. I can buy tomatoes every day of the year, from wherever they are shipped in. Or I can use strawberries, watermelon, beets, pickled green tomatoes from a season past, sautéed turnips, braised kale, or cucumber. Out-of-season produce is downright depressing. Limp asparagus, pale strawberries, mushy tomatoes—an insult not only to the memories of summer's jewels but to the hardy plants that get us through winter. Why would I accept a bland GMO tomato from a greenhouse in California owned by ConAgra when I can make something with locally pickled beets that will taste phenomenal on a dark winter day?

Mediocrity Is the Color of Capitalist Capitulation

Who really makes your favorite foods? It is highly likely that the companies you believe you are supporting are either owned or operated by large food corporations. This is happening in two ways: through the infiltration of food giants into the natural foods sector, and through acquisition of small producers by large corporations, which take over production and keep the trusted label that concerned but unaware customers look for. Some say this is a good thing—that wider distribution of "sustainable" foods is desirable. However, I contend that when those foods are being produced by companies with questionable practices, we are really just falling for parlor tricks while they continue to pillage the earth with the majority of their business. This happens not only when we buy "natural" products from companies that also produce processed foods but also when we buy into the "green" image of businesses that bait consumers with higher-quality products but not higher-quality labor practices or environmental standards. If you are dining in a raw foods restaurant, or even some nice farm-to-table joint where the beef comes from down the road, if your meal is being served by an employee who isn't paid a living wage, then you are not making the best choice possible. If that grass-fed burger is from New Zealand and you are at a table in Wisconsin, there may be a better way to both eat well and support local farmers.

Factory as Farm

This all gets much more complex when even industrial foods enter the picture. Which is why buying local foods and cooking from scratch is so important. Making cereal instead of buying it, cooking instead of filling your freezer with prepackaged meals, buying locally fermented yogurt instead of convenient tubes of squeezable "yogurt"—all of these are ways that you can support a local food system instead of a corporate one. If you don't know the farmer or pickler or butcher or baker personally and have to trust brand names for your choices, you should know as much as you can about the businesses you support, because every packaged product you rely on is another one that can make you dependent on companies that you may not support otherwise. Many food corporations are connected to everything from chemical warfare (Monsanto manufactured Agent Orange from 1965 to

1969) to the mass suicide of rural farmers (over 250,000 farmers in India committed suicide over the last seventeen years, constituting what has been described as both an epidemic and genocide. This spike is related to the introduction of Monsanto's GM seeds, which Indian farmers go into inescapable pits of debt to buy), immigration fraud (Tyson was indicted in 2001 on charges of conspiracy stemming from the smuggling of undocumented workers for employment in its plants) and more. Trusting these sources with something so intimate as your food is a risky business at best. The following are some well-known and lesser-known connections between some popular brands and big corporations. Many of these brands are labeled as "certified organic" or at the very least "all-natural" or "100 percent natural." Some of these brands are probably your trusted family favorites—and you should know who is making the foods you eat. Given the fact that our world is now a corporate dictatorship, the list could go on and on. I will concentrate only on the corporatization of several trusted brands that began as local, artisanal, and traditionally made products. Whether and to what extent you continue to support these brands is up to you, but since they aren't so bold about transparency, I'm going to help them out.

General Mills
Cascadian Farms

Muir Glen
LaraBar

Pepsi
Naked Juice

Kraft
Boca
Back to Nature

Kellogg's
Morningstar Farms
Bear Naked
Kashi

Hershey
Dagoba

Nestlé
Green & Black's

Tyson
Nature's Path
Certified Angus Beef

ConAgra
Alexia
Lightlife

Coca-Cola
Odwalla

M&M/Mars
Seeds of Change

Sara Lee
Aidell's Sausage

This list is by no means exhaustive, as acquisitions are in perpetual motion, with companies being bought and sold and merged every few months. Before your next grocery trip, I invite you to take a peek at the environmental and labor records of the labels on your favorite products (they can be easily found online). If it means you are able to choose between a brand that uses child labor and one that doesn't, I think you'll find it worth the effort.

Monsanto Is Everywhere

It's the stuff of conspiracy theories. The self-described "sustainable agriculture" biotech company that produced Agent Orange, DDT, and bovine growth hormone owns more than 40 percent of the U.S. seed market and 20 percent of the world market, according to Organic Seed Alliance, an agricultural seed stewardship organization. Since Monsanto GMO seeds, especially soy and corn, are in nearly every commercially available food, the company's reach is infinite. Until the FDA requires GMO products to be labeled, there is almost no way of knowing which products stem from Monsanto seeds. Monsanto also manufactures and develops most of the chemical agents applied to crops. It defies centuries of farming tradition by banning farmers who purchase its seeds from saving and sharing them, as farmers have done with seeds for much of agrarian history. Not only does it ban farmers from saving seeds, it also files suit against any farmer found with its genetic material. Let's say there are two farmers—one who uses Monsanto seeds and one who doesn't. A gust of wind carries a few Monsanto GMO seeds downwind, and they plant themselves among the non-GMO plants on the farm next door. Guess what? According to Monsanto, that's grounds for lawsuit on the basis of "patent infringement." In fact, on its website the company boasts of having filed 145 such lawsuits against farmers between 1997 and 2010. Whether these lawsuits were settled out of court, and no matter who came out victorious, days or weeks in court is a drop in the legal budget of a giant like Monsanto, while a small farmer could lose everything defending himself against such allegations.

You probably have Monsanto products in your cupboard right now. Many Monsanto-friendly brands, such as ConAgra and General Mills, even produce natural foods. Knowing which Monsanto products are disguised as natural, even certified-organic foods, will allow you to control your consumption of these products.

Skilled artisan producers are a treasure of every community. By doing things like supporting local bakeries, breweries, and butcher shops, you help keep corporate industry as far from your plate as possible and send a clear message to Big Food that you expect more than redressed and renamed processed foods. It is far more advantageous for each region to have a community of talented food producers who know how to make the best of what is around them than it is to have one producer in some random city shipping product to every grocer in the country. That more-more, faster-faster attitude of traditional businesses practices is an issue of the green food movement. We're talking square peg, round hole here. If we are to truly change this system, we have to step outside the lines we've been told to toe and not follow in the footsteps of Big Food. I'd say it represents a conflict of interest that one monolithic corporation owns organic foods and every biochemical imaginable.

Of course, we all can't avoid these brands. That's not the point. The point is to explain why it's not all about meat. Meat is the easiest thing to eat sustainably. It is easier to say "meat is murder" and debate the issues of the meat industry than it is to figure out how to remove GMO corn and soy from our diets. It sure would be easier to do the latter if corporations were forced to label GMO products.

Hmmm. Who exactly is charge of that kind of thing?

The Green Wall

The United States Department of Agriculture is in charge of our meat industry, and the Food and Drug Administration is meant to oversee the rest of our food system, as well as pharmaceuticals. Let's all take a moment to thank these fine folks for the wonderful job they have done in monitoring our food system!

When it comes to policing the food industry, the USDA and the FDA are either completely and totally inept, absolutely corrupt, or both. They are not doing well at policing any part of the industries under their guard. That is because these entities do not work for us, the people. They work for the "people" fortified through *Citizens United*. In fact, many of the highest positions in the food industry and the USDA and FDA are musical chairs occupied by industry CEOs, who jump back and forth, writing policy to fit the needs of the industry. The 2010 film *Food, Inc.* has a great segment on this problematic overlap.

A recent and notable example of this collusion involves GMO foods and Monsanto. Supreme Court justice Clarence Thomas, in the majority on the decision that allowed Monsanto to prohibit seed saving, was Monsanto's lawyer in the late 1970s. Former secretary of defense Donald Rumsfeld was the CEO of a Monsanto-owned pharmaceutical company, and Bill Clinton advisor Robert Shapiro was the CEO of Monsanto throughout most of Clinton's presidency. It is no surprise, then, that much of Monsanto's growth happened in the 1990s and has ballooned ever since. Margaret Miller, Monsanto's former chemical lab supervisor, who developed bovine growth hormones in 1985, moved to the FDA in 1989. Her first role with the administration was to evaluate the effects of new drugs on recombinant animals. The lucky duck actually got a job reviewing the effects of drugs she had helped to develop. Another Monsanto lawyer,

Michael Taylor, advised the company on the labeling of GMO products in the late 1980s before overseeing the FDA's decision to NOT require labeling of GMO foods as the agency's deputy commissioner and then vice president for public policy. He decided to get the job that would allow him to write the rules about labeling. With all those friends on both sides of production and regulation, it is no wonder Monsanto stomps around the world unchecked.

Smart Kids, the Lot of Them

When our food system was streamlined and centralized to allow for the use of fewer food sources and efficient transport, the food industry was also able to divest in the labor force by replacing humans with machines or by using an undocumented labor force that will accept a paltry wage and subhuman working conditions. This move toward centralization also reduced the number of USDA regulators needed to police the industry. It sure is easier and cheaper for the government to regulate a dozen slaughterhouses nationwide than it is to oversee a dozen in each state. The fact that a dozen slaughterhouses in every state probably seems excessive to most of you is a reflection of how far we've come from the old realities of farming and ranching animals. If every apple had to pass through one of only a dozen locations in the country, apples would be a lot harder to find and a lot more expensive. In regions where animal farming is centered, a dozen small to medium slaughterhouses per state still might not be enough for local farmers to process and distribute meat at a slower pace and on a more local scale. Instead of encouraging small farmers and processors to open more processing plants to more humanely handle the meat produced in our country, the USDA stands as a roadblock to anyone seeking to operate outside of the factory farm framework.

It is understandably difficult to discern the best option when the USDA turns a blind eye to the many grievances against and to the insidious actions of large meat producers and processors. At the same time, the food industry has perfected the art of misleading consumers. Consumers bear responsibility, too, as they demand the same selection at the meat counter in April as in November and a predictable selection of fish in cities far from rivers and oceans. Consumers drive this market. If everyone stopped eating factory-farmed beef starting today, and promised not to eat it again until the industry changes, we'd see some movement. If the USDA and FDA outlawed CAFOs and battery cages and mandated further study and completely transparent labeling of GMOs, we would see some movement. Call me a pessimist, but I'm not banking on those things happening.

The Green Seal Uncovered

By now you probably see that it is not enough to eat "organic" foods. In fact, the biggest booby trap in your hunt for sustainable food is prioritizing that tiny little green-and-white seal that stands for industrial organic. What does the "USDA organic" label really tell you—other than "Please pay three times as much," that is? You probably trust the label because you feel that organic foods are healthier for you and your family. While it is true that food raised without chemicals is probably better for your body and is certainly better for the environment, the label does not speak to every element that decides whether or not an item was produced responsibly. As we've already seen with pantry and grocery items, many packaged foods that are labeled as organic may be produced by companies that operate far from the scale of organic, traditional practices. However, with meat and dairy, the standards of "USDA organic" are even more incomprehensive.

Most of the USDA's standards for organic relate to feed and the use of medications. That really answers only part of the question. A "USDA organic" label doesn't tell you whether the meat was raised locally or transported from halfway across the world, a major consideration when looking for sustainable foods. The sticker doesn't address the humane treatment and slaughter of the animals; nor does it serve as a banner for the company's overall commitment to sustainable practices. The fact that nearly every nationally available organic product is owned by a company with a tarnished environmental record and labor violations, and that spends the rest of its energy producing fake foods, is proof of that.

That little green-and-white sticker is also dubious not only because of the USDA's hypocrisy and conflicts of interest but because of the active undermining of small-farm-driven grassroots action that has been craftily handled by the USDA as it successfully demeans honest small farmers and lauds lying corporations. A farmer outside of Portland who raises five or six lambs for slaughter every year will fight tooth and nail to earn that sticker, yet a farmer under contract from Tyson's Nature Farm brand will have no problem gaining that designation. The amount it costs to have federal agents inspect a farm can put a small farmer in the red for a full season, while a large company like Tyson can buy a small farm, have it inspected and approved, and start raking in the higher profits of organic meats with very little risk to its bottom line. Don't forget, the company has its industrial line to bulk up profits, so whether you choose organic or not, the same wallet gets lined. In the decade since taking over the organic label, the USDA has relaxed organic standards to the point of irrelevance.

One recent example was uncovered in late 2010 by Farm Wars, a website dedicated to saving family farms. It exposes the USDA and FDA for their green-lighting of Monsanto's latest product—Sweetos. Sweetos is being marketed to cattle farmers as a replacement for molasses, which is sometimes added to cattle diets as a nutritional supplement and sweet treat. However, this replacement is being sold to farmers as a way to extend the life of feed, or rather to make cows eat feed that is rotting by covering the smell that would normally make the cow reject the food. "Sweetos is an economical substitute for molasses. Sweetos guarantees the masking of unpleasant tastes and odor and improves the palatability of feed. This product will be economical for farmers and manufacturers of cattle feed," said Craig Petray, CEO of the NutraSweet Company, a division of Searle, which is a part of Monsanto.

The main ingredient in Sweetos is Neotame, which has a similar chemical structure to aspartame—a sugar substitute that has been shown to inflict gradual neurotoxic and immunotoxic damage from the combination of formaldehyde and amino acids. The only notable difference between the two artificial sweeteners is that Neotame appears to be even more toxic than aspartame. For reasons the FDA and USDA have yet to explain, Neotame, unlike aspartame, does not have to be included on the ingredient list of any product made with it. That includes USDA-certified organic and USDA-certified kosher foods made from animals that ingested Neotame.

While Neotame is just an additive to the feed of these cattle, Monsanto is also going after the feed itself. Monsanto GMO alfalfa has already been approved by the USDA. Again, since GMO foods are not labeled or tracked, there is no way of knowing where this alfalfa

ends up. Since it is the main grain of many beef operations, including organic ones, GMO alfalfa has likely
already made its way into our food chain. Even green
market giant Whole Foods recently stepped aside, saying
that "True coexistence is a must" in a letter to customers in 2011 immediately following its decision to cease
opposition to Monsanto's push for GMO alfalfa's entry
into the supply chain. More recently, Whole Foods also
admitted that it fills its shelves with GMO corn products.
Imagine how different this whole conversation would be
if that giant had thrown its weight behind, I don't know,
something like *whole foods*. Instead it's linked hands
with the Green Devil behind closed doors, sealing the fate
of our traditional foods while maintaining its pristine
image as a market for healthy food.

This skillful deception also means there won't be a big
campaign for or against these products because no one
knows what foods they are in and thus can't avoid them.
Unlike Coca-Cola's "Live Positively" campaign, aimed at
convincing us all that aspartame is actually good for us,
or the corn industry's "Sweet Surprise" campaign, which
promises high fructose corn syrup is safe, no one in the
meat industry has to jump through flaming PR hoops to
convince the public of the safety of suspect and possibly toxic ingredients. Until we make it over the hurdle of
even requiring labeling on these items, we will be nowhere
near banning them.

This is but a brief examination of the USDA's lack
of will in safeguarding our food. Clearly, if the USDA

is untrustworthy in its standards for and consistent regulation of certified organic, any other standards the organization sets are just as questionable. The overarching theme is that the rules are set up for the benefit of big business, leaving consumers and small businesses in the lurch. We now have agribusiness companies with over-priced organic lines on the shelves of every grocery store from Seattle to Philadelphia while farmers down the road struggle to recoup the costs of raising their animals well or raising their grains without pesticides with no sticker to show for it. Placing undue and undeserved value on this sticker devalues the intangible, unseen work of small farmers who are exceeding these standards. If you can't trust that prestigious label, what about all the others?

What Do All These Labels Mean?

Many consumers are rightfully perplexed when trying to decipher labels with often overlapping and interchangeable meanings that refer to practices that occur far away from the eyes of any consumer, a fact that is used to great success by the meat industry. How many people purchase "cage-free" eggs believing that the hens laying those eggs are pecking at worms in the sunshine all day? What is the difference between *pastured*, *free-range*, and *organic* anyway? Every level of the industry, from producer to grocery store to restaurant, takes advantage of this cloud of mystery. Transparency is key in sourcing or buying food. You should be able to walk into your grocery store and ask exactly where your meat comes from, and you should be able to get that answer from any person standing behind the meat counter. Simply forming a relationship with a local butcher is a huge step toward being able to trust where your meat comes from. If you can buy your meats from a farmer, even better. However, if you are in a position like most Americans, where you have to go off what is printed on a package, it is even more important to fully engage in decoding the many ways these labels and definitions are manipulated. Only then is it possible to discern between what is truly a healthy and desirable product and something that just looks like one. To appreciate what that means, let's dig into some of these terms and their uses. We must define and distinguish them from one another but also remember that they can be used in conjunction with one another.

All-Natural; Sustainable; Local; Artisanal

These and other terms are really only useful as a reference and mean nothing if not backed up by either regulated definitions or verifiable information gathered through research on a particular product. These terms are not bad; they just aren't enough to go on. Even though I say repeatedly that I source "local" as much as possible, what that means in every instance can be vastly different. It may mean I picked everything up at the market, where foods are coming from up to two hundred miles away. It may mean everything on the menu was grown on the farm hosting a particular dinner, or it could mean the seafood used is from neighboring waters, which could extend politically into the boundaries of several states or even different countries.

All-natural, sustainable, local, and *artisanal* are all subjective terms that you should never take at face value. I appreciate it when diners question my sources. Anyone who has nothing to hide will be proud to explain where every ingredient comes from.

Hormone-Free; Antibiotic-Free

These labels make a few points but miss others completely. The USDA has actually outlawed the use of "antibiotic-free" because this claim implies that an animal never received antibiotics in its lifetime, which is nearly impossible to verify. Many producers still use the label because the meat industry has found it to be conveniently misleading to customers. The "hormone-free" claim is also useless because the USDA allows hormones to be used only in cattle and lamb, so the "hormone-free" label is redundant on any other species. When relying on this label, the package should more accurately read something like, "Synthetic hormone-free" or "rBST-free." Lastly, hormone and antibiotic use are important but minor parts of the sustainability picture.

Free-Roaming, Free-Ranging Poultry

These words are not regulated and are another great indicator that invites further exploration. These terms are often used in regard to poultry. While "free-roaming" birds is a step up from the battery cages that are finally becoming illegal in some states, where birds are cramped six or eight or more to a cage, these birds are far from living natural lives. They are often in huge open warehouses where thousands of chickens waddle around on legs that industrial evolution didn't intend for holding their own weight. Most rarely have any access to the outdoors, despite marketing that claims otherwise. These birds are a much better choice when compared with the sad, diseased, and tortured birds that come out of factory farms. Especially when used in reference to animals such as beef, lamb, and pigs, these terms should be used along with *pastured* or *grass-fed* to really mean anything more than minimal improvement on industrial standards.

Pastured

This unregulated term is often used interchangeably or in combination with *grass-fed*. Usually, if these words are being tossed around, there will be a real, live human of whom you can ask more pointed questions regarding the life and death of your dinner choices. The term *grass-fed* refers specifically to the diet of the animal, while *pastured* refers to the daily activity and living conditions of the animal. Pastured animals are allowed full and uninterrupted access to pastures, fields, and other open spaces. For instance, pastured chickens are what most people picture when they think of "free-range" or "cage-free" chickens. Pecking around for bugs, seeds, and grubs is what chickens are supposed to do. They are not meant to survive on man-made feed, even if it is enriched in omega acids, organic, and soy-free. The rich eggs and meat of such chickens redeems the bland reputation industrial chicken has earned. Pastured cattle graze on fields of grass, and pastured pigs root around for pretty much anything they can find, with treats from the garden and kitchen. This is the storybook farm and the source for the highest quality and most sustainable meat. Pastured meats are often not certified as "USDA organic"—because many farmers simply can't afford or don't pursue the designation and because the requirements of "USDA organic" certification are primarily concerned with feed, which is also required to be certified "USDA organic." Bugs and kitchen slop and brambles are unlikely to ever be inspected and certified by the USDA, yet these are exactly the foods that chickens, pigs, and goats traditionally enjoy, in addition to their daily buffet of grasses from acres of pasture. So meeting the criteria of the USDA requires farmers to continue to buy into the grain-based system of feed. Big shocker.

While the term *pastured* is unregulated, you should be able to verify the claim by speaking directly to the farm or at least to the butcher who buys from and visits said farm. The term *pastured* really just describes an animal raised pretty much exactly as someone would have raised it two hundred years ago. Pastured meats are my gold standard and the base of all my dinners and events. These animals never know hunger, abuse, or any other maltreatment and are assured a quick and painless death that then gives life once more as we nourish our bodies. As Mac Magruder said earlier in this book, "We should all be so lucky."

Grass-Fed

This unregulated term is usually used in reference to beef but can be used to refer to other grazing animals, such as bison and lamb. Sometimes also called pastured, this is the traditional method of raising cattle: grazing them on fields of various grasses. The taste and texture of grass-fed beef varies depending on the breed of cattle, the composition of vegetation available, and other natural variations. In general, though, grass-fed meats are lean and rich in flavor. Grass-fed meats are also shown to be healthier because they typically have less fat, and the fat formed by grazing animals has a different chemical composition than grain-fed meats. Many substances and toxins are stored by animals in fat cells, so the fat of grass-fed meats is also likely to have fewer of these compounds. One stark reality about grass-fed beef is that it is, by definition, a seasonal item in most climates. In Oregon, that season is usually from late spring to early fall, meaning several months of no beef each year, just like the old days.

Grass-Fed, Grain-Finished Beef

The standard in many natural food stores and butcher shops, this is a middle ground between the most sustainable practices and customer demands influenced by the USDA grading system. Cattle are pasture-raised and then finished on grain to add the marbling needed to create beef that can be graded as "choice," the second highest level of quality. The combination of feed sources also solves the supply issue posed by completely grass-fed beef, making this meat available year-round. The USDA's grading system for beef prizes the marbling of grain-fed beef. Thus ranchers who do not finish their pastured beef with grain will merit lower ranking labels than those forcing corn on their steer.

The Catch-22 of USDA Beef Quality Grading

All meat served to the public in this country must come from USDA-approved facilities. In these processing plants, regulators and evaluators assign value to cuts of beef. Marbling of meat, distribution of fat, and the ratio of lean to fat are all factors in the final verdict of labels: "prime," "choice," "select," and grades "A," "B," and so on. USDA-approved beef is graded according to a complex algorithm based on the slaughter age of the carcass, which is determined by comparing physiological characteristics of carcasses because high-volume operations have no way of keeping track of the chronological age of individual animals. The indicators are bone characteristics, ossification of cartilage, color, and texture of the eye of the rib, a tubular muscle that makes everyone's favorite grilling steak. As a calf ages, cartilage becomes bone, lean muscles darken, and tissues become coarser in texture. Cartilage and bone maturity receives more emphasis because lean color and texture can be affected by rough transport, temperature, humidity extremes, and other factors after slaughter. These criteria strongly favor grain-fed, factory-farmed beef. A carbohydrate-rich corn and soy diet encourages the steer to grow quickly, putting on weight by adding fat-laden muscles at an unnatural rate so as to reach slaughter weight more quickly. This diet also induces the desired striations of fatty deposits within and around muscle tissues by which beef is judged. According to the standards of the USDA, so-called conventional beef will always rank higher than that which comes from healthy, free animals. This blatant undermining of small farms does not go unnoticed but is hardly unexpected from an organization run by former agribusiness figures. If we want grass-fed meats, we've got to disregard the USDA's grading system and the ill-informed demand for fat-infused muscles of steer fed an unnatural diet.

As you can see, unfortunately, unpacking the many blunders of the USDA and FDA would take up volumes. It is surely easy to see that looking to either of these entities for help in deciding the best choice for quality or sustainability is a mistake. So if you cannot depend on labels like "USDA organic" or "all-natural," what about all those third-party labels? While it is always important to ask more questions, many of these regulated terms can be quite useful, as they fill the regulatory void left by the USDA and FDA.

Third-Party Designations

Animal Welfare Approved

The Animal Welfare Approved (AWA) label refers directly and specifically to the living and dying conditions of an animal. By many standards, animals with this label must have full access to pasture, must never receive nontherapeutic doses of antibiotics, and must fit a slew of other criteria related to the animal's general well-being. Slaughterhouses that process these animals are also subject to an independent review. See www.animalwelfareapproved.org.

Certified Humane

Like AWA, this label comes from passing inspection with an organization focused on the humane treatment of animals. Rules about beak trimming, size of pig stalls and cages, and so on all mandate a spacious and peaceful life for farm animals. See www.certifiedhumane.org.

American Grass-Fed Certified

This label verifies that a steer was born and raised in the United States (a lot of grass-fed beef comes from Brazil and New Zealand), was never given synthetic hormones or subtherapeutic doses of antibiotics, and was pasture raised. See www.americangrassfed.org.

Food Alliance Certified

This label simply verifies than an animal has never been given nontherapeutic doses of antibiotics—so an animal that gets sick and receives medication is fair game for this label. See www.foodalliance.org.

Marine Stewardship Council

This label is earned by fisheries that use sustainable and responsible practices. This label should be the bare minimum for fish you purchase. Many fisheries with this designation could still use help, but buying from fisheries that are not even attempting to improve their methods condones the rampant overfishing and habitat destruction that plagues our seas. See www.msc.org.

Fair Trade, Direct Trade, or Similar

Many labels and organizations focus on the labor practices of various industries. It is wise to research the criteria of any given trade-approving entity as some have more stringent standards than others. "Direct trade" is mostly a self-assigned, self-governed program administered by a given company, most often dealing in tea, coffee, or chocolate. For exact standards, ask questions in person or research the company via its website. See www .fairtradefederation.org, www.fairtradeusa.org, www .globalexchange.org, and www.equalexchange.coop.

Certified Biodynamic

While the practices and method of biodynamic farms are not regulated across the board, there is a label for farms that meet the criteria of the Demeter Biodynamic Farm Standard. Biodynamic farms emphasize a well-developed relationship to the natural cycles of the earth, plants, and animals. The "biodynamic" label refers to the use of many traditional methods of food production, as well as forming healthy communities and maintaining biodiversity. Not all biodynamic farms seek official certification, so it is advisable to research the principles of biodynamics and to ask questions of any producer claiming to use biodynamic practices. See www.biodynamics.com and www.demeter-usa.org.

Non-GMO Project Verified

The Non-GMO Project has instituted its own research and cataloging of GMO foods. While the group is a great reference, because GMO foods are not currently required to carry labels in the United States, its scope is limited. However, since there is no other process for identifying these foods, this is a good label to look for. See www .nongmoproject.org.

No Brands and No Billboards

By now you've gathered that government and corporate labels can be misleading or untrue. There's always more legwork to do. My final word on labels and packaging is that no brand, no label, and no single practice is a fix-all. To emphasize this, I actually moved away from my early practice of highlighting specific farms. Creating a brand out of a farm is a dangerous mimicry of industrial norms. Corporate allegiance is a deplorable condition that I do not want to see perpetuated in the world of real, good food. We also have to keep encouraging small farmers by sourcing through farms that haven't earned name-brand status. On the same token, I do not endorse any one farm or product, even my own. Once trusted, labels can eventually lull consumers into believing that a company is remaining loyal to standards it touts on its heartwarming label. Rather than believe that XYZ Ranch is the best source of beef today, tomorrow, and always, we've got to check in every once in a while. Before you know it, XYZ Ranch could be owned by a giant corporation.

Now that we've explored the use and misuse of labels, we can move on to a few terms that are often used in the world of good meat. Buying "heritage breed" meats is a good way to eat meat that either carries some of these third-party labels or uses practices that mirror the standards of these organizations. Heritage breeds need you! These are the livestock versions of heirloom varieties in produce. It is worth the time and effort to learn about the many varieties of each animal so that when you see "Icelandic lamb," "guinea hog," or "Delaware chicken," you'll know precisely why it just may be the best meal you've had in months.

Conservation by Consumption

Heritage animal breeds and heirloom produce varieties are the foods our ancestors raised and ate until the introduction of and conversion to industrial farming methods. These animals and plants took generation after generation of selective breeding to come into existence—an evolutionary feat, since many of these varieties of plants and animals predated our understanding of genetics by centuries. Heritage breeds are our direct relation to thousands of years of domestication of certain animals as groups of people developed breeds to fit every corner of the globe. Some animals were bred to withstand certain climates or other environmental conditions. Some were bred for specific qualities in their meat, higher milk production, or fattier bacon; some for purely aesthetic purposes.

While it did take humans to create these breeds, they were not at all like the scientifically manufactured breeds the meat industry now relies upon. They ate a natural diet, whether that meant grass or kitchen scraps or bugs and worms. They produced few young and grew slowly. The meat and other products from these animals usually stayed nearby, bartered with neighbors and sold in the town market. For these reasons, as production sped up, it was quickly apparent that these breeds were not suited to the demand of the new market. Of course, farmers had families to support. The market had changed, and it was only a matter of time before many farmers stopped breeding heritage animals and concentrated on homogenizing breeds for speed of growth and life on the feedlot to remain afloat as neighboring farms industrialized.

Over the decades that industrial meat flooded the market, heritage breeds fell from favor. Now, many of them are threatened by extinction; some are already thought to be extinct. This is a particularly unnerving situation, as these breeds hold all the genetic diversity of domesticated animals. These are not naturally occurring animals, so once the last Mulefoot pig dies, all the genetic variety and specialized characteristics of that animal die with it. Not only is a genetic line lost, but the human line of wisdom it took to develop that breed is lost as well. Biodiversity, or a wide range of genetic material, is a healthy part of any ecosystem, especially one created by humans, such as the world of livestock. We need as many genetic lines as possible to rediversify our industrial breeds and for people in more regions to raise pigs locally.

By purchasing heritage breed meats, we directly influence and support farmers who are rejecting the industrial model and striking out on their own. They do this more intensive form of farming without government subsidies at the risk that no one will buy the fruit of their labor because of the pretty penny it fetches. However, these farmers deserve your attention because the return of heritage breeds is a major factor to solving the equation of sustainable meat. Every farm that is raising and selling heritage meats is one more that IS NOT a disgusting feedlot. The needs of these breeds nearly make factory farming a nonoption. They demand that the farmer revert to old methods of seasonality and biodiversity. All of this requires respect, attentiveness, and a connection to the earth and its cycles. Every farm that is raising pastured animals is another farm that is not buying into the corn and soy subsidy game, and since the animals on these farms dine on mostly naturally occurring forage, there is no need to truck in feed, lessening the demand for the fossil fuels. By raising far fewer animals, these farms also lessen the problem of pollution from waste products and wide distribution.

Because heritage breeds eat the right foods for their species, are given space to live their lives the way nature intended, and are permitted to form familial bonds, these animals are raised by farmers who are deeply committed to their health. Each of these animals represents a significant investment of the farmer's blood, sweat, and tears, and each is treated as such a vessel of energy should be, with reverence. I can only imagine that these animals are much happier, or whatever comparable emotion one is comfortable assigning to an animal, than their industrial counterparts. Many heritage breeds are raised on very

small farms. Supporting these farms bolsters local economies and strengthens farming communities as it fosters
direct relationships with small farmers and provides a
marketplace for farms that produce on too small a scale
to work with even restaurants or farmer's markets. My
favorite lamb farm will never be able to sell anywhere else
since this farmer kills only one or two lambs a year. While
you or I could buy directly from the farm, no market will
take a product that is available only one or two days out
of the entire year. It should also be said that on a culinary
level, the flavor and texture of heritage breed meat should
not even be diminished through comparison to that of
industrial breed meat, even "USDA organic" meat.

Currently, many heritage breeds are available only on
a very limited basis, if at all. But here are a few to look
for in your area, as well as great resources to help you
keep up with new farmers making the switch to this more
sustainable method of farming.

Pork

The main industrial breed is the White Pig. Its gene pool
is often supplemented by the two most commercially successful heritage breeds, the Duroc and Berkshire. The
Tamworth, Gloucester Old Spot, Large Black, Yorkshire,
Red Wattle, Choctaw, Guinea Hog, Mulefoot, Ossabaw
Island, and Hereford round out the rest of the most
well-known heritage breeds of swine. Some of these are
now seen commonly on menus and in natural markets
and butcher shops. However, some are available from

only a handful of farms worldwide. The rarer the breed, the more interested in tasting and buying the meat you should be. Your purchase of a single rare breed pig might make it possible for a small farm to continue raising that breed instead of turning to more mainstream bloodlines. Whenever you come across a heritage breed pig, do yourself a favor and find a way to have a taste. It'll prove why pork is most thankfully not the other white meat.

Beef

There are nearly twenty breeds of heritage cattle, but due to the varying climates and geography of habitats where cattle are farmed, many of these have been unintentionally preserved by the meat industry. The beef industry has capitalized on specialized breeds, despite using industrial methods. Breeds like Angus and Hereford are examples. However, "Certified Angus Beef" is a brand owned by Tyson and should not to be confused with the actual breed, which may or may not be certified. The dairy industry has relied almost solely on the Holstein for years, though the Jersey and Brown Swiss have benefited from recent demand for milk from grazed cows. Some other breeds are the Ayrshire, Guernsey, Galway, and Milking Devon.

Sheep

There are over twenty heritage breeds of lamb. As farmers have differing uses for the sheep they raise, several breeds have been relied upon and thus preserved for the production of wool, meat, milk, and decorative horns. The fact that Americans don't eat much lamb compared to other red meats has helped in lowering the demand for homogenization of genes. The Icelandic, Tunis, Katahdin, Navajo-Churro, Santa Cruz, and St. Croix are just a few of the breeds of lamb you may be able to find.

Chicken

The main industrial breed is the White Cornish Cross. It is funny that one breed is so ubiquitous when there are over fifty heritage breeds to choose from. Sadly, almost half of those are listed as "critical" or "threatened" by the American Livestock Breeds Conservancy, the organization that tracks numbers of heritage breeds in the United States. While many families are not eating them, the trend of raising backyard chickens is doing a lot to help some of these breeds and is a really good way to ensure that your eggs and meat come from a good source. The Delaware, Sussex, Buckeye, Jersey Giant, Wyandotte, and Buff Orpington are just a few of the many breeds one can find at the market or at the hatchery.

꒰ঌ ꒰ঌ ꒰ঌ

There are heritage breeds of every livestock animal: geese, rabbits, ducks, turkeys, horses, goats, and so forth. They all need help to recover population numbers before they are extinct. Ironically, eating them and thereby supporting the farms that sustain them is instrumental in keeping them from disappearing forever. Informative sites about heritage breeds include the American Livestock Breed Conservancy (www.albc-usa.org), Local Harvest (www .localharvest.org), and Heritage Foods USA (www .heritagefoodsusa.com).

Lifting the Green Veil Is Never Waving the White Flag

We've seen that relying on a single dietary identity, such as "vegetarian," is no quick way to sustainability. Burning through the Green Fog will allow you to remove the guilt and dismantle the elitism that keeps what appears to be good food so conveniently out of reach. We now know that good food does not have to break the bank; nor does it have to be placarded with government labels. It is positively frustrating to feel that one's options are limitless in their inefficacy. The system is broken from both ends, and it is up to each of us to hobble together the best solutions we can.

My way of reacting to all this collusion and confusion is to try to source only whole foods from local sources and to make nearly everything from scratch. That works for me because I'm a chef and my life revolves around food. You will have to decide what is right for you. Simple switches in habits, like buying locally milled oats instead of packaged oatmeal from a Monsanto-related company, or buying a whole chicken from the market instead of a bag of drumsticks from Tyson, could be the little change that will make a big difference. Any start is a good start.

We've made it through the hard part. Your blinders are off, and it is time to form your very own food rules. We looked in the mirror and gave up on the diet as personal identity to allow more genuine discernment of our food's merits. We've covered what all the labels mean and discussed sourcing locally. These all answer the questions of *how* to eat and buy food more sustainably. However, for many of you, that still doesn't answer the question of *where* to find these foods. The next and final chapter will point you in the right direction and give the last few tips you need to strike out on your own.

7

The Good Butcher

Italian master butcher Dario Cecchini, who is highly respected as a legend throughout the trade, often says that four distinct elements define meat that can be deemed "good":

1. A Good Life
The animal lived as nature intended, with access to space, fresh air, and the natural diet appropriate for its species.

2. A Good Death
The animal was treated with respect up until its final breath. Death came swiftly.

3. A Good Butcher
Only a skilled hand cut the meat, to maintain its integrity, to obtain the most meat, and to keep valuable cuts intact.

4. A Good Chef
Only a talented cook dignified the animal and all whose labor brought it to that point.

It is easy to see why each of these elements is as important as the next. Every step must be made to ensure that your meal is the best it can be, and any hitch in any given key will take away from that quality. I can cook up a steak of factory-farmed beef, but it wouldn't hold a candle to a hunk of local, grass-fed beef. A farmer could hand me a case of gorgeous heritage breed chickens for processing, and if not careful I could turn those thirty-dollar birds into piles of valueless mangled meat instead of perfect leg quarters, breasts, and so on. All must be in balance, or all is lost. This golden rule is so solid that each of these key elements can be extended to create an excellent means of determining the holistic sustainability of all our food choices. So it is through these four easy-to-remember keys that we will examine the final few points.

A Good Life

We've already covered much of what it means to have a "good" life as an animal in the food industry. It involves an appropriate diet, exercise, social interactions, and gen- erally any other elements that make one's life worth living. Many of these factors can be verified through a simple visit to a farm or by questioning the source. This rule can also be applied to the life of our plant-based foods. A good life for a plant would be one free from pesticides and other chemicals. It is also one that is free from human suffering. Labor abuse and human rights violations are commonplace in the produce industry, so assuring that your food was produced by companies with respectable records on these matters is paramount in assuring a clean conscience.

A Good Death

A good death is one that comes quickly and painlessly. Humane slaughter does not ensure that the animal *enjoys* its death—just that it be kept as happy and calm as pos- sible throughout the process and transition from farm to processing plant. Just like Jim Parker, who gives his pigs trailer rides their entire lives to make them see even their final ride as a fun outing, farmers who respect the sentient nature of their animals work to make sure the inevitable does not become the unconscionable. With seafood, this step would refer to the capture methods, which we want to make sure are the least damaging to the environment. Similarly, we can extend this to our plant-based foods by ensuring that they are harvested in responsible ways and transported minimally. All that effort to raise organic, biodynamic grapes is lost if they are trucked, shipped, and flown across the globe before they reach your kitchen.

A Good Butcher

We've finally made it to the question of WHERE to find good meat. I've waited this long to say it this plainly: Meat you can truly trust comes from a face you can truly trust. You have to know where your meat is coming from, plain and simple. This means buying meat only from a neighborhood butcher shop, from grocery stores with real butcher counters in plain sight of customers (not shady backroom operations), through meat CSAs or buying clubs, or directly from farms through on-farm sales, farmer's markets, or mail order. Whatever the source, the person helping you should possess a wealth of knowledge about meat in general and in particular, and even more about the farms that provide the meat. It is not enough to list the name of a farm. Ask questions about specific practices. The butcher should be able to field your questions with confidence or find someone who can without much fuss. Your butcher should be working from whole animals to the extent space allows, and he or she should be willing to cut meat to order and to your specifications, within reason.

If you can't find a trustworthy shop, forming or joining a meat buying club is a great way to get good meat. Some meat buying groups are informal groups of friends who take turns driving to a farm to pick up meat and animal products to be split among the group. My bacon club was a type of meat buying club, as I made the journey to farms for heritage breed pork so that my customers didn't have to. Community supported agriculture (CSA), a system by which small to very large groups of people buy shares in a farm, or sometimes an individual animal, and over the season receive periodic deliveries of goods, are a more organized version of this arrangement. It should also be noted that many markets accept EBT (electronic benefit transfer), or "food stamps," making good foods accessible even to those who rely on government assistance for food. Some states even double the benefits for those who buy at a farmer's market—so you could go to the market with ten dollars in food stamps and walk out with twenty dollars in local produce. For lower-income folks, a healthy diet is especially important to combat diet-related health issues such as diabetes and hypertension, so this access to fresh, real food is invaluable. Check with your state's food assistance program to find out more about accessing better foods.

Many of the sites listed in the heritage breed section are good for locating farms to source through. CSAs and meat buying clubs can be found through an Internet search or by asking around at local markets and co-ops. The best directory for good butchers in the United States is The Butcher's Guild, a network of sustainability focused butchers, chefs, and meat processors. See www .thebutchersguild.org.

Any company you source food through should respect its employees as well as its customers. Safe working conditions, access to health care, and a living wage for all are integral parts of a holistic, sustainable food system. My mantra here: If you aren't buying from someone who is clean and honest, you are buying from a dirty liar. It might be a bit harsh, but it is true and easy to remember. If a shop, restaurant, or farm is not clean, both physically and morally, and you can't trust information regarding particular practices, they do not deserve your business. They are taking your trust for granted, when it should be earned. I have walked away from meat and fish counters or left restaurants after one too many blank stares and "ummm's" in response to simple questions. I wouldn't have blamed anyone for walking away from me years ago when I was a hapless vegetarian pretending to know meat. If a business appreciates your patronage and cares about change, it will care deeply about filling its ranks with approachable, knowledgeable, well-treated people who are more than happy to answer any questions you have. Thankfully, there are trustworthy farms and butcher shops across the country, so a Good Butcher is never far away.

A Good Chef

The buck stops here. It all comes down to what happens in the kitchen. If you are the cook, well, your job is easy.

When you invest in better food, it makes sense to be nicer to it. If you spend money on a whole pig and you and a friend drive an hour each way to pick it up, you've invested quite a bit before you even think about applying heat. Honor your investment with exciting, delicious preparations and festive, celebratory meals. Branch out and try new flavors and new ingredients and find yourself gaining confidence. As a chef, I feel humbled by the opportunity to elevate and share the work of farmers when I turn their animals into succulent meals. When you eat that twelve-hour pulled pork, the human and porcine energy trapped in each bite is almost a flavor unto itself.

When you put your trust in us, your chefs and food producers, you are indeed taking a gamble with this final key in "good" meat. I believe wholeheartedly that the role of all chefs, food writers, and others in this field is to elevate food, not demean it. We should all take the harmful actions of the food industry as personal offense and seek to not only reverse these irresponsible practices but to distinguish ourselves from the world of dishonest, disgusting fake food. We should be explaining and correcting the deliberate and rampant misinformation and exposing the lies. We should be rescuing our precious baby from the Big Bad.

This role is of utmost importance for chefs and food writers in the spotlight and at the top of the culinary world. Unfortunately, though, money talks, and a disgraceful trend among chefs has emerged. Many reputable and talented chefs now lend their names and likenesses

to the same large food corporations responsible for producing the food that is literally killing the world and
everything in it. It is deplorable for any person who claims
to love food to entice consumers to buy powdered cheese,
microwavable cake, or chemical-filled sausages when they
could be using their talents to show how easy these things
are to make at home. Good food is easier to make than
many think. It is our job as talented food athletes to show
others that they can cook, too. We should be demystify-
ing the act of cooking, not making the fog thicker and
harder to wade through. Though, aside from this more
surface offense of using culinary talent to sell mediocrity,
many chefs are guilty of an even worse grievance.

It is beyond imagination that any chef would use his or
her position to encourage higher consumption of fragile
or depleted resources and unsustainable practices. This
problem is an issue when it comes to seafood in particular. Nearly every food program on TV calls for the use
of seafood items categorized as "red" or "to be avoided"
choices by leading seafood sustainability organizations.
Rather than use their wide reach to educate consumers
on better choices, these shows actually suggest that customers go off into the world requesting items that we
shouldn't even be catching anymore, such as red snapper.
Not to mention that many of the most expensive restaurants source from the same widely distributed commodity
meat suppliers that fast-food chains use. If that burger
costs seventeen dollars, at least make sure it is local and
grass-fed. If it isn't, you are paying only for the ambience.

Despite the fact that the bluefin tuna is listed as critically endangered by the International Union for Conservation of Nature and Natural Resources, it remains popular with many in the food world. An easy Internet search will turn up numerous recipes by Martha Stewart, Mark Bittman, Jamie Oliver, and other celebrity chefs that call for the use of "red" items such as monkfish, skate, and bluefin. Nobu, one of world's best-ranked restaurant chains, proudly serves bluefin alongside the vulnerable and often poached Chilean sea bass, while nearly every well-respected sushi spot lists it, as well as other red-line seafood choices such as yellowtail, sea urchin roe, and *unagi* (farmed eel). Top chefs are making their names on serving endangered sea life and processed foods while lining their pockets with money from companies that strangle the lines that bring good, real food to market. When we've successfully outfished the seas, we can thank them for the great recipes.

"YUMMO" KILLED YUM, or . . .

How Rachael Ray Destroys Good Food in Thirty Minutes or Less

It is scientific fact that every time Rachael Ray says "yummo," an angel loses its wings. In the few years she's been on air, her simple 30 Minute Meals have gone from quick and simple to dumbed down and bland. Her posting of recipes that make use of boxed macaroni and cheese and other Kraft products, which are almost invariably highly processed corn-based products, might have something to do with her role as a spokesperson for Kraft and just might have something to do with her apparent abandonment of all that is good and true in the world of food. Ray started with a good concept. Thirty minutes is actually a perfect amount of time to create a wide range of delicious, healthy meals from simple and even inexpensive ingredients. If you learn the basic rules of cooking and play around a bit, you will always end up with something at least palatable if not downright scrumptious. There is an endless abundance of culinary knowledge that can help us learn how to grow or make anything. Compared to the chemistry of that energy drink your coworker is drinking and the micromechanics of our smart phones, cooking is a walk in the park. Martha Stewart, whom I admire for her dedication to old world techniques, may not always use sustainable products, but at least she keeps it real by making culinary techniques accessible for the home cook. Conversely, Rachael shamefully just proves how bad one can screw up this final stage in the "good" food process. I'm sure I'm not the only food lover who loathes her lamentable creations.

Now, don't get me wrong. I'm the kind of guy who identifies as a capital F Feminist. I don't take lightly the possible misogynist or sexist implications of my assertions about Rachael Ray. Men discredit and dismiss the work of women as a matter of course in the culinary world, as they do in the world in general. I constantly attack the patriarchy of the kitchen, I respect women chefs, and I am in no way attacking Rachael Ray personally. She is an avid pit bull lover and works against dog-breed-specific legislation—both redeeming qualities in my book. She's probably a hoot to hang out with and might even still have a strong cooking bone in her body—when the cameras are off. I guess I just expect more of the gal. Few chefs have attained the level of mass exposure she has. Rachael Ray could have been more like Julia Child. Julia made the exquisite accessible. A chef of her standing ought not to be actively working to eradicate traditional food and food production methods. A chef who is the mouthpiece for Kraft, Nabisco, Coca-Cola, or any similar corporation is a disgrace to her coat.

According to the famous Japanese food critic Yamamoto, a great chef should do five things:

1. Take work seriously.
2. Aspire to improve.
3. Maintain cleanliness.
4. Be a better leader than a collaborator.
5. Be passionate about his or her work.

Rachael Ray and many other celebrity chefs would sadly not pass that test. Thankfully, there are many, many of us who are working ourselves ragged fighting this system. The chefs and butchers I know and respect wouldn't be caught dead tossing boxed macaroni into a dish. I know butchers who would love nothing more than to lock the USDA out of the shops forever. I know chefs who have gotten into physical altercations over what pig farm another chef used. Some of these people were introduced in earlier chapters. It is my joy to share several of the most influential friends I've made in food before closing this final chapter.

These are the people who have shaped the chef and butcher that I am today. But most inspiring of all, they have defined the kind of chef and butcher that I want to become. I am just thirty, a very young chef, and I didn't attend culinary school. But I have learned from and created a food philosophy through watching every chef, butcher, mixologist, cheese maker, and sommelier I've worked with.

Bryan Mayer

I'd be nowhere without Bryan. That first year of butchery started this whole project, and Bryan was there rooting me on from the start. Bryan's salty sweetness introduced me to the culture of butchery and is the soft lining around his exacting standards and meticulousness. I am eternally gratefully that I came up cutting with Bryan, who went on to run Fleischer's Meats in New York after we parted ways. Bryan is opening up his own shop in Philly sometime in 2013. Look him up. A word of advice: Bryan's overall demeanor at any given time can be judged by the state of his facial hair.

Tressa Yellig

Tressa Yellig is the first chef I worked with as an equal, though I was nowhere near her in skill or technique. Tressa and I formed a close working relationship that lasted about a year, doing events together on a regular basis in the space where Salt, Fire & Time, her rad community supported kitchen (CSK), is located in Portland. A CSK is like a CSA, except customers buy shares in the production of the kitchen instead of the farm. Every week, Tressa fills baskets with slow-cooked bone broths, fermented veggies, fresh pâtés, and other homemade kitchen staples. Tressa influenced and encouraged my love of traditional foods and preparations. It was also with Tressa that I began to focus my attention on providing accessible, low-priced meals to the community. She and I spent the entire summer of 2010 serving ten-dollar BBQ plates every Friday night. All local foods, one menu, no reservations, food goes till it's gone. That was the deal. By midsummer we had lines down the block and our BBQs began to feel like family cookouts. I was hooked on that atmosphere, and that free-flowing familial energy is what I always shoot for with my dinners. Tressa's dedication to slow foods and timeless methods inspired me to fully commit to my own vision of what food "ought" to be. Tressa also makes the best kombucha in the world. Go for the rose-cardamom or lemon verbena and be ready for transcendence.

Tessa LaLonde

What does one say about Tessa LaLonde? You have probably never heard of her, but chances are if you've eaten at a top-notch restaurant around the country, you've had her food. Tessa has me beat by ten in the Vagabond Chef contest. She's been traveling the country doing everything from stages at four-star restaurants to working as the private chef for porn stars. Tessa is a whirlwind in the kitchen. I met her several months before I scheduled my first tour, when she volunteered to help Tressa Yellig and me with a few events. Her adventures in chefdom were entirely the inspiration for my decision to become a traveling chef. Tessa also *really* likes to talk about gas. Yours and hers.

Tia Harrison

I always describe Tia Harrison as Superwoman, as I am genuinely convinced that she hides a cape under her chef's coat. Tia is a mother and the executive chef/owner of Sociale in San Francisco, and she co-owns the women-owned and women-run butcher shop Avedano's, also in San Francisco. Tia also cofounded The Butcher's Guild. With my perpetually full plate, it is thinking about Tia that helps me reel myself back in and take one bite at a time, or at least chew those far-too-big bites with my mouth closed. Tia's respect for me as a chef and butcher has been humbling and has pushed me to fully inhabit the niche I have created for myself in the food world. I chose a very different route for my culinary career, one that confuses some of my peers. But Tia has always understood my work, and that recognition became a drive to excel in this world. When you want to master a craft, you must come into contact with those who have mastered it already. Tia Harrison is that person for me. She is also the only person I know who can watch as many reruns of *Law & Order: SVU* as I can. It's our favorite pastime.

Marissa Guggiana

Marissa Guggiana is an author and a fifth-generation meat cutter. When Marissa chose to include me in her book *Primal Cuts* in 2010, I had barely been a butcher for two years. The exposure from her book pushed my work out into the world in a way I couldn't have imagined. Marissa cofounded The Butcher's Guild with Tia Harrison, and together the two of them are truly the vanguard of the Butchers' Revolution. Two lady butchers taking on the meat industry while shaping its future—how could you not love that? I admire Marissa's love of not just food itself but of food culture. We've shared stories of sleeping on borrowed floors before successful events and scraping together our last coins for public transportation to expensed flights and lavish meals. Marissa follows this food trail in much the same way as I do, with a blind faith that this is the only way to Truth. Food is love, food is family, and food is history. Marissa gets that, and she gives her all to help others see it, too. Having just published her third book, Marissa almost makes me think that writing another book is a good idea. Almost.

Jesse Gold

Jesse Gold is one of the most wildly talented chefs I've ever met. Jesse and I founded a radical chef collective in Brooklyn in late 2011 and curated many events together. Jesse not only influenced my cooking but revolutionized the way I think about the kitchen. Jesse was the first chef I met who was interested in deconstructing the patriarchy of the kitchen and the classism of the food world—the first truly radical chef I met. By "radical chef," I mean a talented and visionary chef who is also staunchly against the status quo in all realms of life. Jesse possesses an extensive knowledge of traditional food practices and the medicinal use of foods. While being a pretty hardcore vegetarian, Jesse also supports the consumption of well-sourced meats—a true welfarist. Together with Jesse, I developed the full spectrum of vegan to meat menus for public events that I have now made routine. Our monthly Sunday brunches were all about sating every taste bud in the house and supporting personal food choices. Jesse openly challenges any vegan chef to a game of vegetal prowess called Salad Wars.

∽ ∽ ∽

I have been afforded the chance to collaborate with and document the work of others who are building an alternative market and an alternative food system in response to a standard that rewards shortcuts, fillers, and falsification. I've walked the farmer's markets of cities all over the continent at every time of the year. I know how much work it is to make time in a busy Brooklyn schedule to get down to Park Slope Food Co-op and how lovely it is to live in Montréal with a daily market four blocks away. I've met farmers who operate honor-system on-farm stores and butchers who take the time to share their skills with the community through workshops and apprenticeships. Each of these people has shown another possible way to fix the world's food problems.

This journey has been more than just a formation of my own food ethics. This has been an ongoing opportunity to conspire with the leaders and unsung heroes of the true counterculture food movement.

Even after nearly four years of searching, I'm not ashamed to admit that I've yet to find the best balance of ethics and the realities of the industry; nor do I know everything there is to know about meat sourcing, farming, or the butchery trade. This is a mastery of skills that will take many more years to mold and shape, but knowing how to answer my own questions and how to observe and learn from my peers has helped me connect others to solutions for their own questions. Being invested fully in anti-oppression principles and working outside the capitalist structure doesn't square so well with running a business, and this internal conflict was an early issue that had to be addressed. Financial sustainability has to be part of the "sustainable" foods conversation. If the fancy locavore backyard-garden-sourced café on your street tanks after a year due to lack of customers, high overhead costs, or whatever the case may be, that is indeed NOT sustainable food. Sustainable means "able to continue." I came to learn that lesson personally over and over again because I so strongly wanted my events to be accessible, as well as overflowing with transcendent foods from nearby pastures, that I routinely cut my own profit out of the equation. I wouldn't call that selflessness or revolutionary business principles—just me being naive about how to best marry my desire for a wide audience with my desire for high-quality food. It took me three years in the industry to get to a place where I feel confident about my methods of engagement. I had to learn that what I was creating was not a business venture but a community-based political action centered on open discourse. I had to learn that activism can take many shapes and that political work can have absolutely nothing to do with politicians or the prescribed channels of power.

Over these years and scores of events, I have whittled myself down to a sharper, more accurate point. I understand my work and my role in this world, even as I continue to define it. I am here as proof that all of us can get where we need to be purely by asking the right questions, by never settling, and through downright willful self-determination and self-definition. Revolution is based in the realization that one is not a part of, or benefiting from, the system currently in place—and thus must demolish that system to replace it. Why would we think for one second that the entities that gave us this world, and continue to profit from it, are going to give us the tools with which to dismantle it?

There's an often-repeated slogan among North American protestors and activists: "The system isn't broken. It was built this way."

The systems and cycles of oppression I have been referring to throughout this book—the systematic dishonesty of both industry and government and the befuddling labyrinth that has been put in place to keep the "good life" out of the hands of many—are all proof of this. Animals are not abused because people are mean; they are abused because it takes a long time to raise and kill animals humanely. People aren't refused health care or higher wages because their bosses are evil; they are treated poorly because fair compensation costs more money. Good food is not expensive; bad food is falsely cheap—because it is not really food and is made up of government-subsidized ingredients. Bad food makes people sick, and sick people need medication, so why would natural healing and healthy diets be encouraged by the industries that profit from this cycle?

Yesterday was too late, and tomorrow is never promised. Build your world today.

You've been wanting to quit your job and start a farm or apiary or become a baker—DO IT. You are thinking about trying a raw foods diet—DO IT. You have space for chickens in your yard and your city allows them—GET CHICKENS. You wish you could make your very own two-year-aged prosciutto or just-hot-enough hot coppa—study up for the next three years so you don't poison anyone and then get your *salumi* on. You wish you had time for a garden—start an herb garden in your window and progress to outdoor spaces. Convince neighbors to turn lawns and fallow backyards into plots of food. Make your own pickles and jams.

Practice cooking new foods because eating locally and seasonally will likely introduce you to foods you have never seen before. Go for the bitter greens you've never tasted before or the odd-shaped radishes, the beets with radiating rings of rose or the multicolored duck eggs. Eat breakfast every day so you are never tempted to pull into that drive-thru of factory meat for a calorie fix again. Remember food groups? Vitamins and minerals and micronutrients are things to keep in mind, too. Are the plates of food you are eating full of different colors and textures? If not, proteins, good fats, fiber, and other necessary nutrients might not be present.

Learn to read the signs from your body about what YOU need to eat. How do you feel after meals? Food is fuel and medicine. Propel your gifted machine with foods that both treat and prevent illness. Because of the lack of access to affordable health care in the United States, there are probably millions who must choose between paying medical bills or the grocery bill. The $150 that someone spends every month for hypertension medications just may be partly why he or she mostly relies on fast-food restaurants for meals. That $150 could buy a lot of produce, even overpriced organic. With the guidance of an experienced doctor or nutritionist, many people find they are able to divest money from the pharmaceutical and medical industries and invest in local farms by switching to plant-based diets. Such diets have been proven to treat everything from heart disease to some forms of cancer in studies by doctors in both the United States and China. Most prominent of these is Dr. Caldwell Esselstyn Jr., who was featured in the 2011 film *Forks Over Knives*.

Eating seasonally and locally provides you with the foods needed today, for today's conditions. One eats squash and apples, citrus fruits, dark greens, root vegetables, and bone broths in fall and winter, storing up valuable iron, calcium, vitamins A and C, bioflavonoids, and other immune system boosters. We eat warm, hearty meals that repel the cold and repair the injured and irritated tissues of sore throats, congested lungs, and runny noses. In spring, we see new buds of green in the form of stinging nettles, fiddleheads, ramps, early onions, herbs, and wild mushrooms just as our palates and bellies tire of stews and braises. For me, that little glimmer of green is enough to keep me eating turnips and potatoes for another month or two, because it reminds me that summer's bounty is near. Berries, elderflowers, and roses are just around the corner, and soon after, summer is in full swing. We are outdoors, eating bright salads and snacking on tree fruits, melons, and snap peas. There's wild forage from hiking trips, fish from boating trips, and grills going with chops and cheeks from local pigs. Even as we are distracted with this bounty, the real harvest is yet to come. Late summer and early fall bring us the return for a winter of temperance and months of increasing indulgence with a yield of crops that floods markets well into late fall. Then we are again left with the roots, apples, and squash that can survive the cruelest parts of the year along with us. But if we are smart, and well-prepared, preserves from summer and fall will be there to cheer us up on even the darkest days. Eating with nature is a pleasure and an opportunity for lifelong learning as we regain the wisdom lost over the last couple of generations.

If any of the topics of the last few chapters got you riled up—do more research, find some like-minded people near you, and join the fight! It is not about agreeing on a method of action. It is about being engaged with the search for solutions. There are so many little steps that will help you escape the current. It doesn't matter which ones you take. It only matters that you keep moving.

It is time to break free. It is up to all of us to hone our points, to take better aim, and to continue liberating ourselves and the world. We've only scratched the surface. Name an issue facing the world today, and our food system is likely to be implicated in some way or another. Good food, REAL food is all we need to power the work ahead.

Read up. Teach up. Eat up. Get out there and fight another day. The world is waiting.

Conclusion
We've Only Just Begun

As it encapsulates all that these years have given me, the Ethical Butcher projects rest with this book. My work reaches beyond butchery and meat-focused events. Though my perspective is still always meat-centric, my life in food moved past that some time ago. We do not have the luxury of tunnel vision. I don't want to keep having conversations that are limited to the ethics of meat consumption or local sourcing. I like to have the hard talks. While it was and continues to be an honor to work directly with farmers, I have for some time now been much more interested in working with my community. It is not enough to say that the meats I use come from sunny pastures or to brag about my local raspberries. I want to say I am helping people to eat better, and that takes more than local foods.

As I've said before, we make definitive choices each day. Just as I wake to engage in a battle for a world where women are allowed to make decisions about their bodies and my LGBT peers can walk the streets safely and love freely, I work for a world where we all have the privilege and ability to feed ourselves well. I want to see a world where police don't target men who look like me and collect accolades for maiming and executing unarmed humans, just as I want to see a world where corporations don't collect profits from maiming and torturing animals. Even after reading this book, some of these connections may seem far-fetched to many. I am perfectly alright with that. I don't have time for proselytizing.

In the year since the bulk of the Ethical Butcher projects quieted down, I was lucky to run into more than a few chefs ready to kick up some dust with me. I spent the first half of 2012 forming 718 Collective with Jesse Gold and Cresta White, a pastry chef, herbalist, and massage therapist. Together the three of us sought to create what we called a band of chefs, with the goal of creating a unique reality in the food world, where politics, food, art, and music came together. Our three main objectives—EAT, CULTIVATE, and INTEGRATE—were all translated into community engagement that ranged from pickling workshops and catering for nonprofit organizations to low-cost community meals and raging nightlife events featuring world-famous headliners and our local handmade treats. Ever been to an underground dance party with a Brazilian rapper, edible sculpture, a pop-up vintage clothing shop, and three flavors of homemade ice cream? In April of 2012, about two hundred sweaty Brooklyn hipsters got just such a taste of our collective's ultimate food dream. At some point it became a given that my meats come from local farms, and how many parties could I really throw with that same angle?

When I got to Brooklyn in January, it was a blessing that I found Cresta and Jesse ready to make new moves. We got a great following in our first few months. Brooklyn was hungry for community chefs, and we were flooded with requests. A busy spring culminated in a large collaborative event with a pair of local filmmakers who produce a web series highlighting the activism and art of queer-identified people. The premiere of the web series was a big hit, but we knew that changes were nigh for our fledging collective. As summer of 2012 approached, and with it my thirtieth birthday, I felt a familiar pull. Cresta had a summer of fun with her son ahead of her, Jesse was offered a studio in Texas to record an album under the stage name Dreamboat Crusaderz, and I followed those magnetic tugs and found myself in Montréal, Québec.

Yep, Canada. The wide expanse of land between the United States and the North Pole—a horrid land of universal health care, affordable tuition, and more than two relevant political parties. I could not have predicted it, but this is where the road has led me. I have yet to decide on full expatriation, but the more I watch the news from my new northern digs, the less I feel like returning to the States. My experience of Canada is greatly influenced by the fact that I am living in Québec—French Canada. This is a whole new world, six hours from New York City. Here I can do the work I am most interested in: combining community-based work with an even more defined cuisine. I came here ready to feed a few friends, and I found a home.

Montréal's left-leaning culture is openly anticapitalist. Economic accessibility is everyone's priority, to the extent that pay-what-you-can and sliding-scale cover charges are the norm for social events, concerts, lectures, and other events. The city's network of public swimming pools is free. There's an extensive network of bike paths so it can be free to get around, too. I found that activists here value community building through events, the arts, and political engagement. Old punks own restaurants, and collectively run spaces are the norm. I've seen restaurants that pool tips, kitchens with no head chefs—the list goes on. I knew this was the next stage for me.

A proud French heritage and slight xenophobia mean that a strong local foods scene is a given in Québec. There are five butcher shops within walking distance of my house, and none of them are run by fresh-faced tattooed kids like me, Bryan Mayer, or Tia Harrison. These are old-school joints that haven't moved in decades because Canadian Big Beef never stamped them out the way butchers were wiped away from U.S. neighborhoods.

No gluttonous corn subsidy means far less junk food in stores. There are not one hundred candy cereals to make use of cheap corn. There are not fifty fake fruit drinks filling the aisles. In fact, my favorite comparison of U.S. versus Canadian farm policy is my favorite juice from the grocer on my corner. This particular brand of juice comes in a range of fruit and fruit/vegetable blends, all 100 percent fresh juice. These one-liter bottles are less than two bucks everywhere in the city. What would one expect to find in most U.S. stores for that price? A soft drink or colored corn syrup labeled as fruit juice drink with maybe 10 percent juice. A comparable bottle of 100 percent juice, especially exotic blends, would be at least twice as much. All because corn is cheap. Here, I can go to the market with ten dollars in my pocket and come out with local eggs, produce, and maybe even a bit of Quebécois pork or a few wild foraged mushrooms. I can walk to one corner and buy local beef or cross the street to buy fresh baked croissants. I can trust that the food I buy is real because I can talk to the farmers at my market every day. While I had this accessibility to farmers in New York City's Greenmarket, Montréal's cost of living means I can spend much, much more of my income on gorgeous, seasonal, local foods.

There's an appreciation for originality in Montréal that few cities provide. Montréalers are always interested in newcomers and new ideas. I found a community where I was able to explore and expand my cuisine and was provided with space to create conceptual menus and crazy dream meals at accessible prices. With a few food punks, I discovered ways to push cuisine forward, not for press or promotion but for the fun of it. With a weekly taco night through summer, I served up everything from coffee-rubbed steak and pickled beets to charred green beans and homemade chorizo. Over the successful run of these nights, I also poured on the heat with twenty original hot sauces and salsas. At another spot in town, I was the guest chef for weekend brunch. This is where I really let myself get carried away. Biscuit sandwiches, lemon curd, bacon steaks, BBQ ribs and eggs—anyone who ate my plates over the summer knows brunch is my favorite meal. Among this run of menus was probably one of my proudest culinary feats to date: La Bombe Brunch Burger—a homemade cherry-habanero sausage burger with yellow tomato ketchup on a challah bun with a side of potato donut tots. Yes, a burger and donuts. All handmade; all local. That's not a hangover cure—that's Nirvana.

Our responsibility to be vigilantly engaged with the dismantling of the status quo doesn't end with what is on our plates. We must all continue to vote with our forks, with our legs, with our wardrobes, with the power of our words, and with the integrity of our actions. Through future projects, new collaborations, and progression toward my end goal of providing accessible local foods and ongoing community building, I hope to continue to learn about and reshape the framework that provides structure to our society for all my days.

Montréal offers me a quiet place to collect my thoughts, yet there's enough of a pulse for me to put out plates that let the alchemist chef inside show off while the activist chef does the work. It'll take a lot of convincing for me to settle for another city before I fully explore this one. So if you find yourself in the Great White North, look me up. We'll break bread.

Or bacon.

Acknowledgments

My unending thanks go to every farmer in the world working to keep traditional foods alive and every chef and butcher fighting to bring good food to the table. I am equally grateful to all who have participated in the Ethical Butcher projects and volunteered at events. I especially thank those who supported my very first attempt at getting my work out into the world through Kickstarter in 2010. I never did get that bacon business going, but your support propelled my earliest projects and helped me define exactly what I wanted the Ethical Butcher to be: a politically relevant, community-based project with a cultural and philosophical platform.

I would specifically like to thank Tia Harrison, Stevie Ann, Jade Fair, Lisa Bleviss, Marino Bennadetto,

Ramdasha Bikceem, Melanie Magenta, Cresta White, Sarah Jenny, Keetha Mercer, the Hart Collective, Dirtbag Palace, Hot Lips Lodge, the boys of Original Plumbing, and all the friends and strangers who have housed me over these years of motion. Though it has been some time since I have had anything resembling my own "home," each of you made sure I felt that I had just returned to the nest every time I appeared at your doorstep with my big red backpack. The years that have passed since I first picked up a knife have been a roller coaster of unexpected triumph and unforeseen defeat. Without your helping hands, wise words, and open ears, I would have begged to be let off this ride long ago. I've rarely betrayed my fears and doubts, yet your unfaltering support kept me afloat on the hungriest and darkest of days and enabled me to brave the next round. It will take me a lifetime to thank you fully, but I hope the tangible form this journey has taken will find you. And that you will, in turn, see yourself reflected in its pages. Thanks to Dan Smetanka and the Counterpoint team for helping to create intellectual space for an antiacademic. I promise, there's a lot more where this came from.